Celebrating
Earth Holy Days

Celebrating Earth Holy Days

A Resource Guide for Faith Communities

SUSAN J. CLARK

CROSSROAD • NEW YORK

1992

The Crossroad Publishing Company
370 Lexington Avenue, New York, NY 10017

Copyright © 1992 by Susan J. Clark

Printed in the United States of America
Typesetting output: TEXSource, Houston

Library of Congress Cataloging-in-Publication Data
Clark, Susan J.
    Celebrating earth holy days : a resource guide for faith
communities / Susan J. Clark.
        p. cm.
    Includes bibliographical references.
    ISBN 0-8245-1182-4
    1. Earth—Religious aspects. 2. Earth—Religious aspects—Prayer-
books and devotions—English.   I. Title.
BL438.2.E29 1992
291.1'78362—dc20   92-3748
                                                              CIP

To baby Clare,
and your still-to-be-born siblings and cousins,
may the world you and your children inherit
always flower and sing with the love of your Creator.

Contents

❀

PART TWO
PERSPECTIVES

PART THREE
BUILDING AN EARTH HOLY DAY

PART FOUR
WHO WILL SAVE THE EARTH?

THE FATE OF THE EARTH
A Religious Responsibility

Presently we are involved in a ruinous assault on the planet Earth. Our plundering economy, acid rain, hazardous waste, and chemical poisoning of the land are all manifestations of a pervasive cultural pathology that needs to be remedied. Otherwise we may soon discover that we have lost paradise a second time.

Yet the religious traditions of America have taken no serious notice of what is happening, nor have they offered leadership in remedying a situation that is as devastating in its spiritual aspects as it is in its physical aspects. Although other organizations and millions of individuals are dedicated to defending the Earth and its living creatures, they cannot succeed without assistance from our religious traditions.

Hundreds of thousands of species are being extinguished, including some of the Earth's most gorgeous creatures. Once extinguished these species will never return. Human life will be impoverished in direct proportion to such impoverishment of the Earth.

If we continue our plundering of the planet we will condemn all future generations to live not only amid the ruined infrastructures of the industrial world but also amid the ruins of the natural world itself.

Science has given us a new story of the universe, a universe that needs to be understood as an ever more resplendent manifestation of divine reality itself. This manifestation is especially clear in the genetic bonds of unity that bring together the geological, biological, and human components of the Earth into a single community.

The leadership of religion that created the great civilizations of the past is now called upon to create a new type of civilization in the dawning ecological age, a civilization that will be integral with the ever-renewing transformations of the natural world, a civilization that will hand on to future generations a planet resplendent with life in all its fullness and radiant with divine presence.

THOMAS BERRY

ACKNOWLEDGMENTS

Thanks to Danny Martin for giving life to the idea of an Earth Holy Day, and to Skip Vilas for making the vital connection. Also thanks to Werner Mark Linz, Susan Fisher, Nancy Moshe, Jean Bryant, Linda Ward, Amy Fox, Carl Sagan, John Kirk, Gloria Garcia, Tim Weiskel, Arthur Waskow, Thomas Berry, Conway Leovy, Mike Leach, and John Eagleson. Great thanks is due the Worldwatch Institute for years of well-researched and beautifully written reports on the complex of global environment and development problems. Many of the ideas and facts contained in Part One, "An Environmental Primer," come from Worldwatch publications. Thanks to the United Nations Environment Programme, New York Regional Office, under the direction of Noel Brown, for the example of its annual Environmental Sabbath kits for religious leaders, precursors to this book, and for the use of their materials. Thanks also to the World Wildlife Fund International for permission to use the Assisi Declarations and the St. Francis Interfaith Liturgy.

Efforts have been made to secure permissions for all materials used in this book. If any permissions have been overlooked, a note to the publisher will help us to rectify the problem in subsequent editions.

INTRODUCTION

WHY AN EARTH HOLY DAY?

What place do spiritual leaders have in the debate that's raging among politicians and scientists over the crisis of the Earth? Increasingly, their place is at the heart of it, because it is in our religions that beliefs, ethics, and moral codes have their origins. Because our deepest beliefs dictate our actions, what we humans do to avert the crisis of the Earth begins in our hearts.

People's beliefs about the Earth's resources have caused widespread devastation of our home planet — beliefs in the promise of industry, technology, progress, a better life, a perpetual frontier. These new versions of the holy grail impel humans somewhat blindly toward an abyss as we approach the new millennium. The abyss is the fast degradation of the great systems that have sustained life since time began: the waters, the fertile soils, the air we breathe, and the very quality of the sunlight we bask in. The abyss is untold millions of deaths by malnutrition and disease — more every year.

The irony is that it is our beliefs that can save the Earth. The work of the world's religions is in this realm of beliefs, and here lies the leverage we will need to mount the solutions to the Earth's massive, interlocking problems. They include global warming, ozone depletion, the shrinking of the planet's forest cover and arable land base, damage to lakes and forests by acid rain, the population explosion — and their combined effects on the future welfare of the planet and human society. But how will we transcend the beliefs that got us into trouble and move to new, Earth-informed beliefs that will lead us to sustainable ways of using the Earth's resources?

When the major religious traditions began, there was no perceived Earth crisis, therefore no need to formulate dogma on the subject of humans in nature. If the founders and prophets could see the changes that have happened to the Earth today, perhaps their messages would be eloquent, powerful exhortations to rescue our sacred planet.

The major work of saving the Earth will happen in this holy realm. All actions will spring from beliefs held religiously in one human heart, just as they always have. But it will not happen by itself. Leadership is necessary. A common vision is necessary. Some believe a reformulation of basic tenets has to happen.

No less than the combined force of the world's religions, with their power to educate, inspire, provoke, and motivate, is needed to effect a paradigm shift in the ways people see their world and themselves. The institutions are in place worldwide — the pulpits, the classrooms, the study groups, and cadres of dedicated people with a habit of study.

Add the power of a symbolic day — something the churches, synagogues, mosques, and temples of the world, with their ancient origins, well understand — a day of holy observance dedicated to the Earth. Many of the world's religious holidays have their primal roots in the Earth, as celebrations of the harvest, spring planting time, solstices, and equinoxes. Perhaps today a sacred global holiday is called into being by the Earth's future, as people's spiritual need for a deeper connection to the universe converges with our planet's need for help.

When is Earth Holy Day? Each religious tradition on each continent, in each hemisphere, has its own calendar, rooted in the seasons and in the culture of its people. The concept of one international, interfaith Earth Holy Day is compelling, but, practically, one day of the year need not be formally established for everyone. For the past twenty years, Earth Day, April 22, has been gaining wide popular and political acceptance in the western part of the northern hemisphere. Faith communities in this part of the world have already begun to shape their own Earth holi-days around Earth Day.

A growing number of communities in North America celebrate an Environmental Sabbath, or day of rest, a concept rooted in the Abrahamic religions of the ancient Middle East — Judaism, Christianity, and Islam. This holiday is celebrated on the weekend nearest the annual United Nations–designated World Environment Day, June 5. An ecumenical group of religious leaders introduced the Environmental Sabbath in 1988 under the auspices of the North American regional office of the United Nations Environment Programme, headed by Dr. Noel Brown. Historically an important step in the creation of the Earth Holy Day concept, this work laid an early cornerstone upon which to build.

In October 1991, His Holiness the Dalai Lama of Tibet and the International Coordinating Committee on Religion and Ecology (ICCRE) announced an International Day of Prayer for the Earth, to be held June 6, 1992, in an interfaith ceremony in Rio de Janeiro, Brazil. Its purpose is to call the world's attention to the spiritual aspects of the United Nations Earth Summit, or UN Conference on Environment and Development (UNCED), scheduled for June 1–12, 1992.

For several years, ICCRE and others have worked to create a global religious voice to influence decisions at UNCED, the conference of heads of state that many see as the turning point in the race to save the planet. On June 6, 1992, at the International Day of Prayer for the Earth ceremony, ICCRE will present a draft of the Earth Charter (see p. 172), which includes contributions from religious groups on every continent. This draft is offered as an expression of the world's religious voice, a contribution to the framers of the final UNCED Earth Charter, described in Part Four, a document earmarked to be the "moral framework," upon which sustainable decisions on environment and development can be made.

HOW TO USE THIS BOOK

Use this book to construct your own congregation's Earth Holy Day, or Holy Week, or monthly observance — a time set aside to study the Earth crisis and honor the Earth.

The Environmental Primer (Part One) is a step-by-step tour through the physical facts about the global environmental crisis — the foundation for understanding, beliefs, and action. Yes, the global environmental crisis is complicated, but these are the basics for anyone who wants a relatively easy start. From here you and the leaders in your religious community can expand and soon become informed proponents for saving the Earth. All the facets — problems with the land, air, energy, and water — are intricately linked, and all are caused by human activities. Once we comprehend the horror of what is happening to the Earth, we might be left without a reason to hope. But, as "geologian" Thomas Berry said, "perhaps it's only the religious leaders of the world who can truly understand that in the face of seemingly overwhelming odds, we can perceive a reason to celebrate."

In Perspectives, Part Two, three essays offer a hint of the kinds of conversations that are taking place in this field. They are here to whet the appetite for more such spirited debate, happening now on every side of the issues, on every continent. See Resources, Part Five, for more.

Part Three offers materials for building your congregation's Earth Holy Day, including liturgies, prayers, and other writings, ancient and new, from a range of religious traditions. Use the components to build a liturgy for your celebration. Emphasis is on the interdenominational because the immensity and interdependence of these global problems call for affirmations of our connectedness. As the human species is one people, many races, perhaps our human religion is one God, many voices.

"Who Will Save the Earth?" (Part Four) describes how religious leaders and communities are taking part in the local and global search for solutions. It contains documents central to the spirit and environment movement.

PART ONE

An Environmental Primer

1

EARTH

TROPICAL DEFORESTATION

The Problem: Disappearing Forests

Tropical rainforests cover only 7 percent of the Earth's land surface, yet contain two-thirds of all plant and animal species. Tropical forests form a lush green band around the equator, concentrated in three great blocks — the Amazon Basin in Latin America, the Congo Basin in West Central Africa, and the Malay archipelago between Southeast Asia and Australia. Enormous resources exist there, which are being lost. Despite a surge in international concern, our forests are disappearing fast, with an area at least the size of Pennsylvania cleared every year. Because of loss of habitat following deforestation and desertification, the Earth may lose forever as many as one million species by the end of the twentieth century.

Developing countries are home to nearly all the world's tropical forests, a category that includes jungle, rain forest, cloud forest, and swamp and mangrove forest, covering an area about two-thirds the size of South America. Since developing countries are the poorest, they can least afford the costs involved in halting deforestation.

In Part One I have relied heavily for scientific material on Walter H. Corson, ed., and the Global Tomorrow Coalition, *The Global Ecology Handbook: What You Can Do about the Environmental Crisis* (Boston: Beacon Press, 1990); Lester Brown, et al., *State of the World: A Worldwatch Institute Report*, 1987, 1988, 1989, 1990, 1991 (New York: W. W. Norton, 1987–91); Cheryl Simon Silver and Ruth DeFries, *One Earth, One Future: Our Changing Global Environment*, National Academy of Sciences (Washington, D.C.: National Academy Press, 1990); and World Resources Institute, United Nations Environment Programme, and United Nations Development Program, *World Resources 1990–1991: A Guide to the Global Environment* (New York: Oxford University Press, 1990).

Causes

Third world debt is indirectly responsible for forest loss. Encouraged by northern banks and driven by the need for economic development and growth, developing countries borrowed heavily at high rates of interest when oil prices skyrocketed in the 1970s. To pay off the debts, they rely on exports of primary products unsustainably extracted: timber, minerals, and agricultural and forest products.

Misuse of agricultural land leads to loss of forests. In many societies, the forest was traditionally slashed and burned to clear it for farming, but then it was left unplanted for thirty-year periods to return the land to forest and allow it to regain its fertility. Because of rising populations in rural areas, land is often not left fallow; it is quickly brought under cultivation, which degrades the land so that its return to forest is no longer possible.

Commercial plantations of crops for export are replacing forests. Among the crops are bananas, coffee, rubber, oil palm, cacao, and, in Peru, Bolivia, and Colombia, marijuana and coca for cocaine.

The world's appetite for timber is another cause of deforestation. Logging continues, even accelerates, in all three tropical forest blocks. Tropical hardwoods bring precious cash needed to pay debts. Half of all logs are exported, with Japan and the United States the biggest customers. Timber for fuel razes vast tracts. Brazil, for example, uses timber as fuel to fire twenty iron smelting plants in the Amazon.

Although logging in itself does not cause deforestation, it scars the land, and 55 percent of forest that is logged over eventually becomes deforested. Logging roads open up previously inaccessible areas to settlers. Careless logging can destroy forests: in Borneo (now Myanmar) a forest burned for four months in 1983, destroying timber valued at $6 billion.

Overharvesting fuel wood and fodder leads to loss of forests. The timber taken for fuel wood and charcoal is roughly eight times as much as is extracted by logging. Wood is used for cooking and heating by 80 percent of the developing world, half the world's population. Overpopulation, landlessness, and poverty are major causes of overharvesting.

A quarter of tropical forest loss worldwide is due to the clearing of land for cattle ranching. Government policies often encourage this unsustainable practice in the mistaken belief that it is the best route to earning foreign exchange. The practice is driven by demand for meat in developed countries. Cleared grazing land is productive for only a short time; then its value is lost.

Large-scale development projects such as hydroelectric dams, roads, and agricultural settlements destroy forests. Land is cleared by burning, which releases carbon dioxide into the atmosphere, adding to global warming.

Population growth and unequal distribution of land in tropical developing countries contribute to destruction of forests. In developing nations, most fertile land is owned by a few wealthy landowners (in Latin America,

These Sudanese children are environmental refugees, the victims of drought. They are traveling from the Red Sea Hills Province in Sudan to seek refuge in relief camps. Photo: Maria Antonietta Peru, UNICEF.

7 percent of the people own 93 percent of the land). Landless people are forced to clear forests and farm marginal land. Landless people who flee to cities often are resettled on cleared forest land, as in Indonesia and Brazil.

Military operations can destroy forests. A prime example is the defoliation of Vietnam's forests, which have not recovered. One third of the country is still wasteland. Wildlife is lost; the productivity of cropland and fisheries is depressed.

Effects

The loss of forests has widespread implications for all people. Indigenous peoples lose their homes, food supply, and cultures. Many die or are killed. Lost also is their knowledge of sustainable forest management and of the medicinal or commercial properties of many forest products.

Deforested soil can never again support a tropical forest or even grow crops for long, because most of the land's nutrients are in the vegetation, not the soil. The land eventually becomes barren and useless.

Deforestation threatens the natural balance of upland watersheds. Rainwater can no longer accumulate in vegetation and soil for slow release, but washes past in floods, eroding soil. In Bangladesh, for example, downstream from deforested northern India and Nepal, the flooding is devastating.

Drought and crop failures follow. Reduced water flow through cities threatens contamination and disease.

Soil erosion causes siltation of streams and rivers, which kills fish and damages downstream estuaries, mangroves, and coral reefs. Navigation is hampered, and the useful life of hydroelectric plants is shortened.

Deforestation destroys habitats for uncounted species. Since the thousands of species in a tropical forest are interdependent, loss of a few species can snowball into mass extinctions. Migratory bird populations, for example, are declining dramatically, and deforestation in the tropics is the major cause.

Tropical nations lose future revenue from the sale of hardwoods and other forest products when forests are destroyed instead of sustainably managed. Although thirty-three developing countries are currently net exporters of forest products, only ten are expected to be so by the year 2000. The world is already seeing the beginnings of fuel wood and timber shortages.

Loss of forests causes alteration of regional and even global climate patterns. Regions become drier and the planet's weather changes. From the rain they receive, forests produce water vapor, which rises to become clouds. When the rainforests are gone, the rains stop. Forested lands are dark, and so absorb incoming sunlight; deforested areas are light and reflect the sun. This change in brightness (albedo) of the planet causes convection (air movement) patterns to change globally.

Loss of the genetic potential in the forests is permanent. Deforestation is happening at the brink of a revolution in genetic engineering that could yield an unimagined bounty of answers to the world's food and medical problems. But genetic material is lost through deforestation, even before many of the forest species can be studied. Products could bolster the economies of developing nations, provided adequate arrangements are made with the biotechnology companies that develop them.

Solutions

To be successful, programs to set aside forest reserves must include involvement by local and indigenous people and consideration of their needs. Provisions must be made for local benefits from tourism, agroforestry, and watershed protection.

Better management and protection of forests by developing nations require sustainable logging practices or even outright bans on timber exports. Nations themselves can maintain and control harvesting of forest products for export, tasks usually performed by foreign logging companies. They can develop their own facilities to process wood for a better income than from the sale of raw logs to developed nations (trade agreements permitting).

Many areas of Europe, once severely deforested, have been replanted, proving reforestation can work. China's reforestation efforts finally paid off in 1985 with reforestation of over 3 million acres, a net gain in forest cover that year.

Practices by development projects that erode or deplete soil must be prevented or curbed. Small-scale, community-based projects, such as agroforestry projects, are increasingly favored by development agencies. Such agencies should encourage efficient, sustainable forest management and cattle ranching.

Improved agricultural methods, such as intensive and multispecies farming and management of pasture lands, can reduce the land taken over for farming. More intensive, efficient methods of raising cattle can do the same.

Consumers in industrialized countries could reduce demand for tropical products that destroy forests: paper, beef, coffee, tea, rubber, coca, sugar, and palm oil. Ideally, prices would go down and pressure on forests would decline.

Individuals can help by becoming educated and joining some of the thousands of nongovernmental organizations working at the grassroots level to protect forests. Environmental groups concerned with related issues such as global warming, depletion of species, and social justice for indigenous peoples can be effective in pressing for reforms.

Land reform in Third World countries would reduce the number of people who must clear the forest for subsistence farming. Ruling wealthy elites traditionally favor the unreformed status quo.

Governments can reverse or correct policies that subsidize cattle ranching and agriculture on cleared forests and policies that price timber below value. Integrated programs of health care and family planning are needed to ease population pressure on the forests.

Debt-for-nature swaps, that is, the cancellation of foreign debts for agreeing to create forest reserves, have been successful. Conservation International, an environmental group based in Washington, D.C., arranged a landmark debt-for-nature swap in 1988, when it paid off $650,000 of Bolivia's outstanding debt (which had been discounted to $100,000 by creditors doubtful of receiving full payment). In exchange, Bolivia designated a 3.9 million acre buffer zone of forest and grassland around the Beni Biosphere Reserve in the Amazon Basin, creating an endowment fund in local currency to manage the land.

New plantations can take the pressure off natural forests. In Brazil, for example, 14 million of the 50 million cubic yards of wood used annually for charcoal production and fuel wood consumption come from eucalyptus plantations. But in most countries new plantations are not being established nearly fast enough.

A Tropical Forestry Action Plan to tackle deforestation on a global scale, costing $8 billion over the next five years, will in the long run prove to be a profitable investment. Development agencies and governments are partially funding the plan and cooperating to implement it.

DESERTIFICATION

The Problem: Encroaching Deserts

Desertification is the spread of desert-like conditions following the erosion, compaction, salinization, and/or waterlogging of the soil, which is in turn followed by loss of the land's biological productivity. Most often, land in arid and semiarid zones desertifies. Agricultural land loses its productive potential, sometimes permanently.

Desertification threatens the world's dry lands, about 35 percent of total land area. The dry lands support 850 million people who produce meat, cereals, fibers, and hides. About three-quarters of the dry lands are already desertified to some degree, and the livelihood of those 850 million people is seriously threatened. Two hundred million others would be affected by desertification of the dry regions.

Every year about 21 million acres of land are irretrievably lost to desertification, and a further 52 million acres are so degraded that crop production does not pay.

Causes

Desertification is a symptom of underdevelopment, a combination of social and economic factors, such as the inequitable distribution of resources and inappropriate land use systems. Desertification occurs in semiarid areas more often than in arid areas. Where rainfall is moderately reliable, the temptation is to grow crops, such as livestock feed.

Population growth is a major indirect cause of desertification. Feeding more people every year strains agricultural and grazing lands. Overgrazing by livestock and deforestation for fuel wood leads to degradation of soils and watersheds.

Salinization and waterlogging of overirrigated land are also common causes. Others include the expansion of intensive cash cropping onto marginal land more suitable for animal grazing, poor management of boreholes to water stock, and the settling of previously nomadic peoples.

When farmers burn animal dung and crop residues for fuel instead of allowing them to enrich the soil from which they came, soil fertility declines, vegetative cover decreases, and soil erodes. The moisture-holding capacity of the soil then weakens and the whole system collapses.

Droughts accelerate desertification and amplify its effects. The Sahel has undergone four major droughts in the twentieth century: 1910–15, 1944–48, 1968–73, and 1982–84. The last two droughts caused widespread loss of human and animal life because conditions had previously deteriorated.

Effects

Desertification played a role in the downfall of the Sumerian, Babylonian, Harappan, and Roman civilizations. Salinization occurred wherever irrigation flourished. In what is now Iraq, irrigation was accompanied by rapid population increases in 1800 B.C.E. and 900 C.E. Populations sharply declined because of desertification that followed waterlogging and salinization.

Today about 8.5 billion acres of land, an area the size of North and South America combined, are affected by desertification. Two percent of Europe, 19 percent of North and South America, 31 percent of Asia, 34 percent of Africa, and 75 percent of Australia are at risk from desertification. At highest risk are large areas of Africa and parts of California, Chile, Argentina, northeast Brazil, Iraq, Pakistan, Turkey, Spain, and northwest Australia.

Desertification takes the form of encroaching dunes and sand sheets, deteriorating croplands and rangelands, destruction of tree and shrub cover, or deterioration in quantity or quality of ground and surface water. Fertile land near the edges of existing deserts is at highest risk. Aerial surveys over the Sudan reveal that the edge of the Sahara, marked by the disappearance of subdesert scrub and grassland, moved southward about sixty miles between 1958 and 1975.

To produce enough food to outpace population growth, agriculture depends on expanding land area under cultivation. But partly because of desertification, limits have been reached in many parts of the world. Irrigation, responsible in part for dramatic gains in productivity, also causes salinization, waterlogging, and ultimately desertification. Worldwide, food production per capita has been declining since 1970.

Solutions

Technical solutions such as reforestation, improved farming techniques, and better land management have had limited success in reversing desertification. Land can slowly recover, once pressure is removed — providing enough good soil remains in place and local climates do not change radically. In the Amazon of South America, for example, farming the rainforest could be replaced by low-input, sustainable farming of the savannas (tropical grasslands). But recovery can be so slow that the damage is, in effect, irreversible.

Part of the solution is to develop hardy crop varieties that use nutrients efficiently. Triticale is part rye and part wheat, with the best properties of each. It does well in acidic, salty, or low-manganese soils. The Armadillo variety of triticale is a recent improvement, but so far is suitable only for unleavened breads. New research promises further improvements, including a strain for use in leavened breads.

A total of $141 billion would be needed to curb desertification of rangelands and agricultural land. The sum is approximately equal to the estimated loss of agricultural production dependent on deforestation over a five-year period.

The most successful attempts to control desertification have been inexpensive, small in scale, and planned and operated by those personally affected. In spite of some successes, the battle is being lost. A massive new effort to control desertification is required if declining productivity, erosion, famine, and consequences such as political chaos are to be avoided.

2

AIR

❦

We now see that the air, the ocean and the soil are much more than a mere environment for life; they are a part of life itself. Thus the air is to life just as is the fur to a cat or the nest for a bird. Not living but something made by living things to protect against an otherwise hostile world. For life on Earth the air is our protection against the cold depths and fierce radiations of space.

— James Lovelock

Pollution of the air is changing the chemistry and patterns of the Earth's atmosphere. It is widely believed to be altering the Earth's climate, causing changes to the Earth's protective ozone layer, creating health problems in cities, and killing forests and lakes. The three major manifestations of the changing atmosphere — global warming, acid rain, and ozone depletion — are caused by emissions of chemicals into the air. The causes and effects of all three are interlinked.

GLOBAL WARMING

The Problem: Global Warming and the Greenhouse Effect

The Earth's heat and energy come from the sun. Most of the sun's energy is bounced back again, out to space, but not all of it. Like the glass in a greenhouse, the Earth's atmosphere, made up of gases, blocks some of the outgoing energy on its way to space. Then the atmosphere radiates this blocked heat energy back to Earth. This is the way the atmosphere normally prevents the Earth from growing too cold for life to survive. The greenhouse effect becomes a problem only when the atmosphere blocks *too much* outgoing heat.

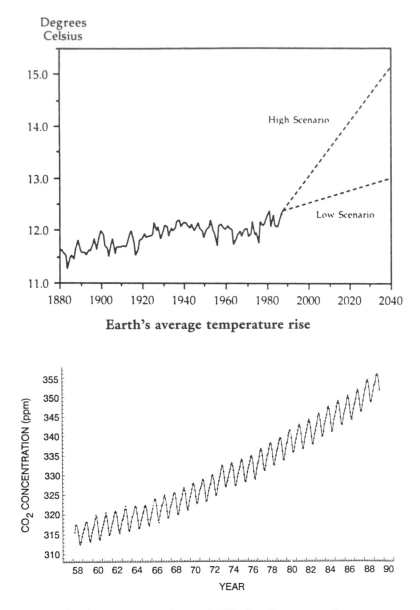

Earth's average temperature rise

Rise in concentration of CO$_2$ in the atmosphere

**Rising in parallel: CO$_2$ concentrations,
global average temperature, and fossil fuel burning**

The Earth's average temperature has risen nearly one degree Fahrenheit during the last hundred years. There is evidence that the warming may be accelerating: the five warmest years in recorded history occurred in the 1980s. The same hundred-year period has seen a 25 percent rise in carbon dioxide concentration in the atmosphere, as measured at the Mauna Loa Observatory, Hawaii. Fossil fuels have been burned in greatest volume during the last hundred years. Note that the two charts do not cover the same time periods. The sharp rise and fall cycle in carbon dioxide indicates yearly seasonal changes. For sources of the data see p. 189

Currently, the Earth is heating up faster than at any other time in its history. The normal composition of the greenhouse shield is changing as humans add carbon dioxide and other gases. The amount of carbon dioxide in the greenhouse layer has increased by 25 percent in the past hundred years (the time we have been burning fossil fuels in greatest volume), increasing the average world temperature by between .36 and 1.08 degrees Fahrenheit. Globally averaged sea level is estimated to have risen by five inches or more. Scientists believe that today's carbon dioxide level will double in sixty years. A likely scenario is that the Earth's average surface temperature will rise by between 2 and 9°F by the year 2000.

Causes

The chemistry of the atmosphere has changed because of rapid expansion of human activity in industry, energy production, transportation, and agriculture, requiring the burning of fossil fuels (oil, coal and natural gas, formed eons ago from decomposing vegetable matter). Fossil fuel burning releases carbon dioxide into the atmosphere.

Global industry operated by business firms based in the developed nations of the northern hemisphere has released enough carbon dioxide and other greenhouse gases to boost the heat-blocking power of the atmosphere. We are actually changing the ability of our planet to cool itself, at rates that can damage the global ecosystem. Each year five billion tons of carbon are injected into the atmosphere by fossil fuel burning.

The large-scale destruction of forests for timber, fuel, conversion to agriculture, and economic development also increases carbon dioxide in the atmosphere, in two ways. Burning and decay of the biomass itself adds carbon dioxide to the atmosphere. And, since living trees absorb carbon dioxide, their destruction leaves more carbon dioxide free to add to the warm-up. Deforestation adds another 0.4 to 2.5 billion tons of carbon to the atmosphere each year.

Carbon dioxide, the most important of the greenhouse gases, is only half the problem. The other half is a combination of other gases — methane (from livestock, landfills, sewage treatment plants, rice paddies, oil and gas wells), nitrous oxide (from high temperature combustion, soil bacteria), and chlorofluorocarbons (CFCs, chemicals used in refrigeration, air conditioning, cleaning solutions for electronics, the manufacture of styrofoam, and aerosol spray cans; CFCs are better known for their role in depleting the ozone layer).

Other greenhouse gases in the atmosphere are present in much lower concentrations than carbon dioxide, but they are accumulating faster. Scientists calculate that over the next half-century or so, the temperature rise produced by increasing concentrations of carbon dioxide will be matched by the effect of the other greenhouse gases, several of which have a more powerful greenhouse effect than does carbon dioxide.

The concentration of carbon dioxide in the atmosphere currently increases by 0.05 percent per year, and methane by 1.0 percent. Because the Earth and its atmosphere are a closed system, venting our wastes does not get rid of them. If greenhouse gas concentrations keep rising, the world's average temperature can rise at rates between ten and fifty times faster than during the ice age recovery period to a high temperature unprecedented in human history.

Effects

Most scientists agree that increasing amounts of carbon dioxide and other greenhouse gases will cause warming. The changes will have major but unpredictable effects on climate, natural ecosystems, and agriculture.

Scientists estimate outcomes by making assumptions about how much of each gas is likely to be released into the atmosphere and feeding this data into supercomputers that model the atmosphere's behavior. But uncertainties still exist, especially about the effects of clouds and the oceans.

What will the temperature rise mean? The significance of a small increase in temperature can be learned from history. The Earth's last ice age lasted a hundred thousand years and ended ten thousand years ago — the time taken by the planet to recover and change to the relatively comfortable conditions we enjoy today. Yet during that ice age, when parts of the northern United States were under a mile of ice, the Earth's average temperature was only 9°F colder than today's average.

A global average temperature rise of only 5°F could mean local increases of more than 18°F at high latitudes in some seasons. In temperate zones winters would be shorter, warmer, and probably wetter, summers longer, hotter, and probably drier; water supplies could diminish sharply. Subtropical regions might become even drier than they are now, and tropical ones even wetter. Rainfall would be affected. Warmer air would cause evaporation rates to increase, and overall rainfall would probably rise.

As the oceans warm up and expand and polar caps break apart or melt, sea levels will rise an estimated three feet over the next century, possibly much more later, leading to severe flooding over low-level land, with intrusions of salt water into coastal groundwater supplies.

Ecosystems that cannot adapt fast enough to regional changes in weather patterns would lose species, entire forests-full. Patterns of agriculture would change. Extremes of temperature would affect mortality rates and could force large-scale migrations.

Global climate change is the most disturbing of all the human-caused environmental disruptions on several counts. Its tremendous scale includes the oceans, the polar caps, cloud cover, and the agriculture of every continent. Specific effects are difficult to predict and, once in motion, could be impossible to stop. The scale of human suffering that is projected — from storms, droughts, floods, and a range of other disasters — makes climate change the overarching global environmental concern.

In 1988 North American crop yields fell below consumption for the first time in history. The same year heat waves in China killed hundreds. The decade of the 1980s was the hottest on record. These and widespread droughts in the early 1970s and continued drought in the African Sahel are the types of changes we can expect with the global warming. Whether it is under way already is under study.

Solutions

Half of all global warming is caused by the burning of fossil fuels for energy. Alternatives to our present high consumption of fossil fuels are discussed on p. 38.

World governments need to formulate policies to achieve three major goals: to prevent emissions of greenhouse gases; to compensate for the emissions, for example, by replanting forests (which absorb carbon dioxide); to adapt to inevitable change.

Protection of the Earth's atmosphere is a major topic on the agenda of the Earth Summit (the United Nations Conference on Environment and Development, or UNCED) in June 1992 in Brazil.

ACID RAIN

The Problem: Ecological Destruction from Acid Rain

Industrial smokestacks and motor vehicles spew polluting gasses, including sulfur and nitrogen oxides, into the atmosphere, where they combine with moisture to become sulfuric and nitric acids, falling to the Earth as acid rain, acid snow, and acid fog. Acid precipitation is only part of the large-scale air pollution problem, which causes regional and even global increases of noxious gases.

Causes

People depend on heavy consumption of goods and energy, not only in the rich industrialized nations of the northern hemisphere, but also in underdeveloped but rapidly industrializing countries like China, India, and the eastern European nations. The role of developing nations will likely increase without controls and the transfer of clean-burning energy technologies.

Acid rain has become a problem only in the last century, paralleling the tremendous growth in industry, energy production, and motor vehicle use. For example, the acidity of precipitation has quadrupled in the northeastern United States since 1900, paralleling increased emissions of sulfur and nitrogen oxides.

Effects

Acid rain seriously damages waterways, soils, and forests, and corrodes buildings, bridges, art, and automobiles. The most important ecological effect is widespread forest dieback, most serious in Europe. Damage has been found in thirty countries, with the greatest harm in Scandinavia, Central Europe, and eastern North America. Fish have disappeared from over four thousand lakes in Sweden; 80 percent of Norway's lakes are classified as "dead."

Acid rain damages entire ecosystems. It can damage tree roots, block nutrient absorption, and make trees less likely to survive drought or infestation. It leaches nutrients from the soil and can cause the release of toxic metals into streams and lakes, killing fish and other water creatures and eventually disrupting entire food chains. The cost of damage to timber and agriculture, to buildings and priceless art, to forests and aquatic ecosystems, and to tourism, adds up to hundreds of billions of dollars. Acid rain combined with ozone and other air pollutants may reduce agricultural and forest productivity by 5 to 15 percent over large areas.

Since acid rain can travel hundreds of miles before falling to Earth, political tensions grow among nations. Norway estimates that 90 percent of its acid rain originates in neighboring countries. Evidence shows that acid rain is damaging the health of the Inuit peoples of the Arctic circle as well as their environment and wildlife.

Solutions

Like global warming, acid rain is caused by the burning of fossil fuels for energy and transportation; solutions to our present dependence on fossil fuel burning are discussed on p. 38.

The long-term solution to acid rain is to reduce emissions of sulfur and nitrogen oxides from coal-fired power generating plants. The European Community has agreed on a plan to reduce emissions of SO_2 (sulfur dioxide) by 60 percent and NO_x (nitrogen oxides) by 40 percent by 1995.

Short-term solutions to limit acid-rain damage include neutralizing acidic fallout by applying limestone, sodium carbonate, and other alkaline compounds over soils and into waters.

OZONE DEPLETION

The Problem: Ultraviolet Radiation from Ozone Depletion

A fragile layer of ozone in the stratosphere, between seven and thirty miles above the Earth's surface, protects the Earth from the sun's damaging ultraviolet radiation (UV-B); that protective ozone shield is essential to life.

Scientists have discovered that a hole appears in the ozone layer over the Antarctic during spring in the southern hemisphere each year, when the ozone shield is routinely observed to be 50 percent thinner than normal. Newer data shows that since 1969 the ozone layer has thinned worldwide an average of 2 or 3 percent, and as much as 10 percent, varying widely by region. This thinning is much more drastic than originally believed. As a result of the hole and the thinning, all life is now exposed to higher levels of harmful ultraviolet radiation.

Causes

Chemicals produced by industrial activity are released into the atmosphere, where they chemically accelerate the breakdown of ozone. This process has been known since 1974, but its damaging effects were discovered only in 1985.

The worst offender is a group of chemicals called chlorofluorocarbons, or CFCs, used in refrigeration, air conditioning, the manufacture of styrofoam, electronic equipment cleaners, and other industrial applications. Other gases that deplete the ozone layer are nitrous oxide and halons and those containing chlorine, fluorine, and bromine. Once in the atmosphere, the active lifetime of the ozone-depleting chemicals is on average one hundred years.

Effects

Effects of ozone depletion on human health are increased eye cataracts and skin cancers, including deadly melanomas; a 5 percent thinning of ozone in mid-latitudes would allow enough additional ultraviolet radiation through the atmosphere to increase incidence of skin cancer by 10 percent. Increased ultraviolet radiation may also damage immune systems.

Increases in radiation could lead to smaller timber and crop yields and damage to marine ecosystems.

If current patterns of industrial activity continue, ozone levels in the upper atmosphere will continue to fall during the first half of the next century.

Solutions

Solutions to the problem lie in reducing and eventually stopping production and use of CFCs and other ozone-depleting chemicals. Less damaging substitutes will have to be used, especially in refrigeration, air-conditioning, and other areas where CFCs are in wide use.

In 1987 the Montreal Protocol treaty was signed by thirty-one nations, including the United States. Its provisions specify reducing the production of CFCs by the year 2000. Further international action is planned that will restrict and ultimately ban the use of the most seriously implicated chemicals.

3

FIRE

❦

The Problem: Energy for Human Use

Of all human activities, the production of energy has the greatest impact on the environment. The world's economy is based on the burning of fossil fuels (oil, coal, and natural gas) for industry, for heat and electricity in homes and offices, and for transportation. Burning these fuels produces carbon dioxide emissions, accounting for half of the greenhouse gases that cause global warming. Fossil fuel emissions also result in the killing of forests and lakes by acid rain and in air pollution, which harms the health of humans and other animals. Of the fossil fuels, coal and natural gas are the most abundant, but burning them causes carbon dioxide emissions. Natural gas is the cleanest-burning fossil fuel.

Reserves of oil, the energy source used by most of the developed world, will, at present rates of use, last only another hundred years, some say less. But energy demand has increased dramatically in recent decades and will continue to rise. The developing world will make major demands for energy as their economies and populations grow. By 2020 the world will use 75 percent more energy than it does today.

As nations exhaust their own oil reserves, reliance on Persian Gulf oil fields increases, and the political and military cost of this dependence goes up. Oil price fluctuations have the power to disturb countries' economies; ultimately people and the environment suffer.

Most developed nations have large-scale, centralized energy systems fueled by huge coal- or oil-burning power plants. Costs of maintaining security for these metropolitan power grids are high and growing.

Other fuel sources have problems as well: nuclear power plants currently carry unacceptably high risks of contamination by radioactive waste and their by-products add to the danger of nuclear weapons proliferation; large hydroelectric plants flood valleys, dislocate people, and eliminate entire eco-systems; and the use of wood for fuel causes deforestation and desertification in developing countries.

Causes

The world is addicted to oil. Rates of energy consumption have risen continuously since the industrial revolution. Over the past forty years, world oil consumption has increased sixfold, and world energy consumption has increased fourfold, with North America using a disproportionate share. With recent exceptions, profligate use almost universally is the rule. Conservation and efficiency are not widely practiced. For agriculture and transportation, there are few readily available substitutes for fossil fuels.

Fueling high energy demands are a near-universal belief in an expanding global economy and a willingness to ignore the environmental costs of carbon dioxide and other harmful emissions.

Effects

Major environmental effects of our energy consumption are global warming (see p. 29) and acid rain (see p. 33).

Moreover, boom and bust cycles in today's energy markets can destabilize the world's economy, with devastating impacts on the environment. In developing countries, because technology for other fuel sources is lacking or expensive, precious foreign exchange is spent on imported oil, using funds that could be spent to curb environmentally harmful industrial practices or to manage water and land resources properly. Dependence on oil imports is a major source of Third World debt, a problem intimately linked to environmental problems.

Solutions

The challenge is to reduce our reliance on fossil fuels, both to stop carbon dioxide emissions and to help establish energy security worldwide.

We can reduce our consumption of goods and fuel. Individuals can conserve energy by reducing electricity use in homes and adopting lifestyle changes that result in fewer automobiles driven for fewer miles. People can buy less and avoid excessive packaging. Recycling saves some of the energy used to manufacture an item and saves landfill space used to dispose of it, but not purchasing the item in the first place saves much more.

We can encourage energy conservation, efficiency, and the use of cleaner-burning fuels: in industry, buildings, power-generating plants, and in transportation. Since motor vehicle emissions contribute to global warming and acid rain, we should step up research into alternative-fuel vehicles, enact stricter controls on emissions, require cleaner burning fuels in urban areas, and extend mass transit systems.

Governments can focus energy strategies on resources within national borders. A system of financial incentives, such as tax incentives and fuel pricing, can encourage energy conservation and efficiency. Taxes on carbon-based fuel emissions offer an efficient way of correcting the failure of the market to value accurately resources such as clean air and the atmosphere's heat-trapping potential. Now in use in many nations, eco-taxes such as gasoline taxes are effective when they are part of an overall plan of partial substitution for income and sales taxes. They promote more efficient energy use while also stimulating the switch to renewable resources.

We can encourage use of alternative energy technologies, those that do not rely on fossil fuels and are based on renewable sources, for example, solar power, biomass, geothermal power, small-scale hydroelectric projects.

Clean, renewable solar energy is the most evenly distributed energy resource available. Many technologies are promising, including power from the wind (solar in that it is caused by temperature differentials across the globe's surface). The photovoltaic solar energy cell turns the energy of the sun directly into electric current. Now nearly cost-competitive with traditional sources, photovoltaics could reduce reliance on power transmission lines, making it an ideal technology for developing nations.

Although nuclear power does not emit carbon dioxide or pollute the air, the risks are high: nuclear accidents with environmental and human health effects lasting for generations; dangers inherent in stockpiling plutonium and nuclear wastes; nuclear materials terrorism.

Grassroots movements can pressure governments to find safe ways of meeting the world's energy needs. Public outcry led West Germany to rule out nuclear expansion in the 1980s. Hydroelectric dams in India have met with public protest, persuading the government to rethink its policies. Fifteen countries have plans to cut carbon emissions.

Aid to Third World countries can focus on environmentally sustainable economic development, including energy systems that do not produce carbon dioxide or other harmful emissions.

A transition to alternative energy systems will create jobs and compensate for those lost in old energy sectors such as coal mining. The business generated by implementing energy-efficient solutions can produce more employment, on average, than finding and using new fossil fuel energy sources.

Nearly every solution is a political solution. The challenge to world leaders is daunting. The truly dire consequences of global changes such as global warming are in some cases generations away. Remedies are expensive in the short term and may be appreciated only by our children's children. Heads of state must consider the web of costs and benefits in a long-term context.

International cooperation is crucial. Progress resulting from the United Nations Conference on Environment and Development, with climate change central to the entire agenda, points toward an international treaty.

4

WATER

❧

THE OCEANS

The Problem: Overharvested Fisheries, Sick Marine Ecosystems

Oceans and coastal zones cover two-thirds of the Earth's surface and contain nearly as many species as the rainforests. The quality and productivity of marine ecosystems are threatened by three major hazards: overharvesting; construction and development; and pollution.

Harvests are dangerously high. The total world fish catch is nearly at the sustainable limit. Fisheries, with depleted populations of marine life, are yielding less in many parts of the world, and some have been completely stripped. Between 1950 and 1970, the world's fish catch more than tripled from 21 million tons to 66 million tons. Some whale species are near extinction.

World food supply is at stake. Seafood supplies over half the populations in developing nations with 40 percent or more of their total protein intake. Of the total marine catch, a third is used to feed animals and fertilize croplands.

Estuaries, where fresh water rivers meet the ocean, trap and retain pollutants rather than carrying them out to sea, exposing marine life and the harvest for humans to ever-increasing concentrations of contaminants.

Many coral reefs are severely damaged by soil erosion runoff, the dumping of waste from dredged harbors and rivers, coral mining for building materials, and the stunning of fish with dynamite or cyanide. These reefs normally support more kinds of life, including one-third of all fish species, than any other ecosystem. Also, where reefs are damaged, there is less protection from storms and beach erosion.

Worldwide, thousands of miles of mangrove forests, which support a rich variety of life, protect from storms and erosion, and filter out pollution, are being destroyed by development, rice farming, and aquaculture farms.

Plastic litter from domestic garbage, fishing supplies, and cargo wrapping is found in every ocean, harming and killing marine life and affecting the beauty of beaches.

The greenhouse effect may warm sea water and expand it, raising sea levels from twelve to forty inches. It could cause weather and wind patterns to change, followed by changes in ocean currents and locations of fisheries.

With a thinner ozone layer, a higher portion of ultraviolet light reaches the oceans. This biologically harmful radiation can harm or kill phytoplankton, microscopic organisms that form the base of the marine food web. The nutrition shortage would have reverberations throughout the global food web. Also, because phytoplankton take up carbon dioxide, reduced levels would mean more carbon dioxide in the atmosphere, exacerbating the greenhouse effect.

Causes

Human activity is responsible for nearly all that threatens marine life and ecosystems: the dumping of municipal sludge and sewage; industrial waste discharge; urban and agricultural runoff; inland deforestation; building and development along coasts; oil spills and discharges of oil from ships; dumping of toxic and hazardous wastes; ocean dumping of dredged material; discarded plastics; and wasteful fishing methods.

Coastal waters are more polluted than the open ocean, because two-thirds of the world's people live along coastlines and rivers draining into coastal waters. Human sewage is the major polluter of coastal and ocean waters. In the United States alone, 3.3 trillion gallons of sewage were dumped into the ocean in 1980. Most American harbors are badly polluted. Sewage sludge can poison species with disease-carrying micro-organisms and pathogens, pesticides, PCBs (polychlorinated biphenyls), and heavy metals. It also stimulates excessive algae growth.

Dredging harbors, channels, and rivers brings up large amounts of contaminated sediment containing oil, grease, heavy metals, and PCBs. Most ocean dumping is of such dredged material, which kills and poisons marine life.

Most oil pollution comes not from spills but from washing out oil-carrying ships with seawater and releasing the oil-laden water to the ocean, causing harm and death to fish, seabirds, mollusks, crustaceans, and mammals.

Women draw water from a traditional well in Missamana, Guinea, in Africa, where water is scarce and often polluted. Photo: UNICEF/Maggie Murray-Lee.

Effects

Yields from fisheries are diminished because of overfishing in earlier years. Oyster harvests in the Chesapeake Bay are less than a third of levels in the 1960s. Major fisheries in the North Sea, the Northwest Atlantic, and on the Peruvian coast have declined or collapsed.

Blooms of algae deplete water of oxygen and damage or suffocate marine life, a process called eutrophication. Some algae are toxic and can poison fish and move up the food chain to larger mammals, including humans. Red, green, and brown tides are algal blooms that can kill vast amounts of sea life. Acid rain contributes to these algal blooms.

Some whales have been hunted nearly to extinction. The Antarctic population of the giant blue whale is 1 percent of its original level; humpbacks are at 3 percent. Despite international outrage, Japan and Iceland continue to hunt whales.

The cancer-causing industrial chemical PCB drops into the ocean from the atmosphere and accumulates in the bodies of sea mammals, impairing reproduction and threatening extinction in some species.

Up to two million seabirds, a hundred thousand marine mammals, and thousands of other sea creatures die every year after eating or getting tangled in discarded plastic. The source is garbage and household waste dumped by ships, fishing vessels, and military vessels.

Sewage from urban areas dumped into the sea causes bacillary and amoebic dysentery, cholera, typhoid and paratyphoid fevers, salmonella, gastroenteritis, and other diseases, depending on the health of the population involved. Hepatitis has been linked to contaminated seafood. Disease-causing viruses have been found to survive for seventeen months in sea water.

Illnesses and deaths among people in England and France have been linked to the ocean dumping of radioactive nuclear waste.

Solutions

A region's marine resources could be managed as an ecosystem rather than simply for the maximization of production of commercially valuable species. To protect ocean fisheries from overharvesting and sustain marine harvests for the long term, agreements must be made that set and enforce fish catch quotas. Minimum net size should be established to prevent the taking of fish too small for commercial use.

The practice of leaving discarded fishing nets to drift freely in the oceans, which trap and kill marine life for many years, should be controlled. Control should also be established over driftnetting, a commercial fishing method using a forty-foot-deep net stretching for thirty to forty miles, sometimes called a "death wall." It catches everything in its path, including tons of sea life not intended for the commercial catch, which is nevertheless killed and discarded.

Fish farming, or aquaculture, can be expanded, especially in Third World countries, where the practice can help solve food shortages, provide jobs, and earn foreign exchange. Improvements can also be made in reducing fish wastage.

Important treaties and conventions have resulted from international efforts to control pollution and protect marine environments. The Law of the Sea Convention recognizes that the oceans are a "common heritage of mankind." It provides that nations must protect and preserve their marine resources for the common good of humankind. Some nations (including the United States) have not agreed to share the mineral resources in deep seabeds, nor to the notion that nations have complete economic sovereignty over the oceans within two hundred miles of their coasts. After nearly twenty years of meetings, nations have yet to agree on a comprehensive treaty covering a range of issues such as fishing, mining, pollution, navigation.

In 1973, nations formulated the International Convention for the Prevention of Pollution from Ships, an agreement known as MARPOL. Among its other provisions, it declared illegal the discarding of plastics into the ocean by ships of signatory nations or in waters of signatory nations. The London Dumping Convention, implemented in 1975, bans the dumping of certain black-listed substances and in 1983 established a moratorium on ocean dumping of low-level radioactive wastes. Regional treaties such as the 1974 Regional Seas Program (notably the Mediterranean program) under the United Nations Environment Programme and the Helsinki Convention of 1974 (for the Baltic Sea) have been successful in cleaning up regional seas.

FRESH WATER

The Problem: Shortages, Pollution, Poor Management

Supplying people, industry, and agriculture with all the water they want is depleting and damaging the world's fresh water supply.

The Earth's limited supply of fresh water is a renewable resource, but only if managed properly. Only 2.6 percent of all water on the blue planet is fresh, with 77 percent of that amount frozen in polar ice caps and glaciers (safely away from polluters).

Heavy and inefficient use of water by humans is draining the world's underground reservoirs at rates far too fast for them to be replenished. Some of these vast aquifers are becoming permanently polluted by contaminants from industry and agriculture. Shortages of safe water in some areas may reach crisis proportions. Agriculture uses the most water; domestic use accounts for 6 percent of total consumption.

A quarter of all the people in the world and half the people in the developing world (about 1.2 billion people) have no access to safe drinking water or adequate sanitation facilities. By the year 2000, many nations will have half as much water per capita as they had in 1975.

Water shortages, especially where nations share river basins, lead to conflict and even war. Forty percent of the world's population is supported by two hundred major river systems. Negotiated trade-offs and cooperation are needed.

Wastes from humans and animals and chemicals from industry and agriculture are contaminating natural ground and surface waters in irreversible ways that threaten future generations' survival prospects.

Even the best water systems have been found to be contaminated by toxic substances. In the United States, where water supply is among the best protected in the world, a 1988 study found 2,100 chemical contaminants in the drinking water. Of these 1,900 had never been tested for adverse health effects; 97 were known carcinogens; 82 caused mutations; 28 caused acute and chronic toxicity; and 23 promoted tumors.

Industry is by far the biggest polluter. Sources of industrial water pollution include the chemical and plastics industries, the metal finishing, iron, and steel industries, the pulp and paper industry, metal foundries, and petroleum refineries.

Contaminants accumulate over time in the bodies of fish and shellfish, often resulting in high concentrations in seafood.

Urbanization in developing countries means denser populations in megacities, where scarce water and lack of sanitation already threaten the safety of the water supply and the health of millions. There, management of water resources for the future is a high priority.

Destruction of coastal wetlands, usually for development, endangers fresh water supplies, since the wetlands act as natural water purifiers. Water development projects such as dams and canals degrade water quality and contribute to disease by providing ideal conditions for insects, snails, worms, and other disease carriers. They can also dislocate human populations and disrupt — even destroy — ecologies.

Acid rain likewise has done significant damage to our fresh water supplies (see p. 33).

Causes

Population growth leads to increased demand for water for energy plants, food crops, and the production of more manufactured goods. Eventually shortages occur. Population pressure on rural lands, especially in Africa, where subsistence farming can lead to dried-out land, leaves future generations with no water supplies at all.

Worldwide, agriculture accounts for 73 percent of water use. Irrigation systems globally are only 37 percent efficient, as water is lost to evaporation and seepage. Water use for agriculture represents more than 80 percent of the total used in the United States; irrigation of pasture land to grow food for livestock accounts for 50 percent of all U.S. water use.

Too much water is being withdrawn from underground aquifers, too fast, often causing subsidence of overlying land, resulting in sinkholes and permanent contraction of the underground basins.

Industry and power-generating plants use vast quantities for steam production and for cooling. When power stations draw water for cooling and return the warmed water to its source, the result is called thermal pollution. The warmer water holds less oxygen, and as a result entire regional ecosystems can be thrown out of balance.

Deforestation reduces soil's capacity to hold water; rainfall rushing across the denuded land carries soil and silt into reservoirs, threatening water supplies and the functioning of dams and hydroelectric projects.

In the production of oil and natural gas, underground aquifers are often contaminated or destroyed by saline water. Acid drainage from coal and other mines contaminates and makes many streams uninhabitable. This pollution increases as demand for energy grows.

Runoff from agricultural lands carries residues of pesticides and fertilizers, harmful to human health, ecosystems, and marine life. These often carcinogenic chemicals pollute groundwater worldwide, posing threats to human health.

Untreated human waste is the world's most dangerous pollutant. In addition, because livestock produce five times as much waste as humans and twice as much organic waste as industry, sewage runoff from ranches, stockyards, and farmlands can also be harmful.

Most storage and disposal of hazardous waste is inadequate. All methods have the potential to contaminate groundwater. Rainwater flows through wastes stored in all but a small fraction of disposal sites, leaching contaminants into groundwater. Runoff from sources such as mines, farms, and urban streets are difficult to trace and remediate.

Effects

If proper water resource management is not practiced, water shortages will limit growth in agriculture and industry and threaten health and economic well-being in most of the world's nations.

Unsafe water and poor sanitation are linked to 80 percent of all human disease. Included are trachoma blindness (500 million sufferers), elephantiasis (250 million sufferers), diarrhea (which kills over one thousand children every hour, eight million per year), cholera, typhoid, infectious hepatitis, poliomyelitis, schistisomiasis, and intestinal worms. All waterborne diseases claim 25 million lives per year; of those, ten million succumb to intestinal diseases. In rural areas entire village economies can be ruined by disease.

Irrigation leaches minerals from soil, leaving water more salty than seawater in some rivers. After extensive over-irrigation, land is left infertile, useless, and glistening with salt, especially in developing countries.

Solutions

Nations must give highest priority to reducing the amount of water that is wasted by industry, mining, electric power production, municipalities, and agriculture. Sewage treatment plants can make best use of innovative, cost-effective methods to improve efficiency and effectiveness of treatment. Aid agencies can lead developing countries to take advantage of lessons learned in the developed world.

Education about hygiene and sanitation, to be effective, must accommodate traditional cultures and customs. Because women are the de facto environmental managers of most of the Third World, women must be directly involved in planning and implementing rural water development programs.

Industrial firms must take responsibility for their part in polluting the world's water systems. For example, the Minnesota Mining and Manufacturing Company (3M) operates a successful program for industry, demonstrating how to conserve water, reduce pollution, and save money.

Governments can curtail irrigation subsidies and other policies that allow agribusinesses to waste water and can instead give incentives to use efficient irrigation methods and reuse wastewater. Farmers and agribusinesses can be led to choose fertilizers and pesticides that are safer (both for ecosystems and for humans) than those being used now. Priority can be given to regional watershed management, incentives that encourage conservation and efficiency, such as pricing water high enough, and legislation that promotes recycling.

Individuals, landlords, and building managers can make household water conservation simple by installing inexpensive water-saving devices such as efficient faucets, showerheads, toilets, and clothes washers.

The United Nations Drinking Water Supply and Sanitation Decade, launched in 1980, has had limited but significant success. Estimates show that 79 percent of urban people and 41 percent of rural people have access to clean water; 62 percent of urban and 18 percent of rural people have sanitary facilities.

5

PEODLE

PEOPLE

❀

The Problem: Global Population Growth and Dwindling Resources

The projected growth of the world's population is thus likely to be a major force affecting virtually every aspect of human and social development, natural resource and environmental management, and economic progress, particularly in the developing world, over the next half century.

— World Resources Institute

Overpopulation and runaway population growth underlie all environmental problems, because it is human activity that is causing degradation of the Earth.

By 1800, after about two thousand years of recorded history, the Earth's human population reached one billion. It took another 125 years to add the second billion, 35 years to add the third, 14 years to add the fourth, and only 13 years to add the fifth, in 1987. The Earth presently supports 5.4 billion people, but unsustainably. We are destroying the resource base that is needed by generations to come.

We add an average of 95 million people to the Earth's population every year, which will amount to another billion by the end of this century. By 2025, according to United Nations projections, 8.5 billion people will vie for the Earth's dwindling resources. Population may eventually level off at 11.6 billion, the theoretical carrying capacity of planet Earth.

In developing countries, where 80 percent of the world's population lives, 96 percent of the world's population growth will take place. The fastest growth is in the poorest areas. The total international debt of low-income nations is $100 billion, making it difficult for them to provide social services for existing millions, yet the need increases for education and health care.

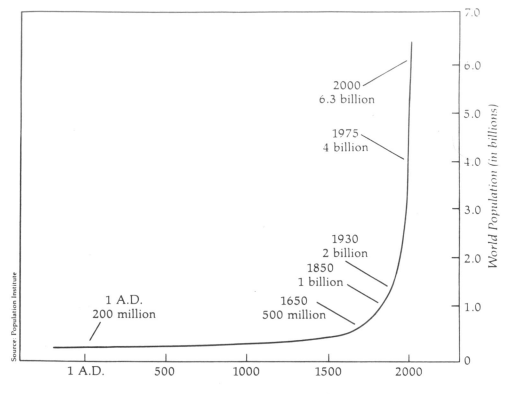

World Population Growth

It is misleading to look only at birth rates. In the late 1970s, the United Nations announced that the world's annual population growth *rate* had reached its high point and was starting to diminish. But dramatic projections for population growth remain unchanged because the absolute numbers will still continue to rise as predicted into the twenty-first century.

Family planning, the most intimate of subjects, has become a political issue for some government leaders. The United States reduced funding for international population agencies on the grounds that the funds could be used for abortions or related activities. As a result, even in countries where abortion is legal, those people who want family planning help (about 50 percent in developing countries) do not get it. In China, a government-mandated one-child policy results in widespread fear, distrust, and even infanticide of girls because of preference for sons.

The population explosion is an urgent reality, yet some religious leaders have trouble acknowledging it. Humanity has a choice: curb population growth humanely or let nature carry out its own gruesome population control program consisting of crop failures (due to global warming), malnutrition, mass starvation, epidemics, and early deaths by the hundreds of millions each year, mostly in developing countries.

Causes

The initial population explosion came about after World War II through the combination of continued high birth rates and a rapid and sharp one-time drop in death rates, resulting in suddenly large populations of children. Ideas and technologies affecting health, sanitation, education, medicine, and education took effect in the developing world after World War II, causing death rates in Latin America, Africa, and Asia to plummet. Before the war, both birth rates and death rates were high, but the number of births per thousand people only slightly outnumbered deaths per thousand, and populations grew slowly. Now, it will take generations before birth and death rates can be brought back into equilibrium.

Even though population growth rates have peaked everywhere but in Africa and the number of children born per woman has decreased, on average, world population will still continue to rise rapidly until well into the twenty-first century, the result of past rapid growth and the enormous number of women who survive to childbearing age.

In the developing world excluding China, 40 percent of the population is under age fifteen. In parts of Africa nearly half is under fifteen. Because far larger percentages of children live in the developing world than in the

Scavenging through trash heaps is a lifelong occupation for many Egyptians, including these children in Cairo. UN Photo 148,016/Jean Pierre Laffont.

developed world, with their reproductive years still ahead, the number of births and the total population will continue to rise.

The greatest environmental damage is done by the neediest and the greediest. On the greed side, the most damage is done by the industrialized countries and the top billion richest people, because of high rates of consumption and use of imported resources in addition to their own. On the need side, the bottom billion, living in the worst poverty, are driven to use resources faster than they can be replaced, just to survive: trees are cut for fuel wood; marginal lands are farmed; air and water are polluted.

Effects

Expanding population is linked in complex ways with all environmental problems. Depletion of soils forces subsistence farmers to migrate to urban centers by the millions in developing countries. These displaced rural people arrive in already densely packed megacities surrounded by slums and shantytowns plagued with pollution, poverty, disease, and social problems.

Coastal zones are destroyed as rural populations mass to coastal cities such as Manila and Bombay, which are growing at 4 percent per year. Air, land, and water are polluted; waste overwhelms cities' ability to cope.

Land resources become degraded when already small landholdings are divided among more children per family in each generation. In fifty-seven developing countries, nearly 50 percent of farms are less than 2.5 acres. In Indonesia, the figure is 70 percent. In Kenya, the average size of farms halved while population has more than doubled. Where there is denser population, there is more soil loss.

Quality of life declines and human suffering rises in countries with continued high birth rates. Most of the deaths in civil wars since World War II have been in developing countries with high birth rates.

From 1980 to 1986 in developing countries, annual carbon dioxide output caused by deforestation tripled, carbon dioxide emissions from industrial use rose sixteenfold, and energy consumption grew 4 percent a year (ten times faster than in industrialized countries). All of this is related to population increase and all contributes to global warming. More people consuming manufactured goods also raises the output of chlorofluorocarbons (CFCs), which contributes to ozone depletion.

Feeding the world's people will depend upon a 50 percent increase in land cultivation by 2025, but today's land area under cultivation may be contracting because of various forms of degradation.

One-third of the world grain harvest goes to animals for dairy and meat products. But even if food resources were used more intelligently, only about one billion more people would be fed, and a billion additional people will be on Earth by the end of the century.

It is not only people who are wearing out the Earth, but also people's animals: four billion livestock and nine billion domestic fowl. Cattle release methane, a powerful greenhouse gas. Raising animals for food uses more land and fuel per unit of nutrition than does growing food crops for direct human consumption.

Destruction and even extinction of species results when habitats are lost to deforestation, desertification, erosion, grazing, and human development of wetlands as a result of human activity. Population growth and migration patterns in parts of Asia may be responsible for up to 80 percent of species loss.

The effect of overpopulation on the environment is an international issue of increasingly major proportions, as insults to the global commons (air, water, arable land base, food supply) grow more severe. Environmental refugees from deforested, desertified, eroded, and depleted lands flee across national borders, straining international relationships.

Solutions

People can learn to make the population connection. Most wars, deforestation, desertification, global warming, many refugee situations, water shortages, and a host of other problems have population pressure as a major component. The relationship between overpopulation and unsustainable development is strong and clear. As people and institutions recognize that the Earth has become a full occupancy planet, they can learn what it takes to slow population growth, and commit themselves to doing it.

A fast-growing population has a multiplier effect on every form of environmental degradation. When governments understand the long-term effects of population growth in their countries, they will integrate projected population growth data into policy making. For example, integrated health care and family planning pay dividends in the well-being of communities and entire regions. Research shows that birth rates eventually decrease as standards of living rise. Because population growth swallows up most gains in development and social services in Third World countries, reducing population must go hand in hand with development.

Nations need to become acutely aware of the dangerous balancing act between population levels and the Earth's resources. Although China's authoritarian methods and one-child policy are harsh, the Chinese example proves that a country's disastrous demographic future can be altered by government policies and programs.

Fertility rates have declined by more than 50 percent between 1960 and 1987 in eight countries in East Asia and Latin America, thanks to wide availability of contraceptive methods, public education on responsible parenthood, government commitment to population stabilization, and broad-based economic and social development.

More women worldwide are reporting that they prefer smaller families.

Nature imposes a harsh birth control policy on humankind when planned birth control fails. Poverty claims this abandoned seven-year-old, one of ten million abandoned children in Brazil, picking garbage in a dump near São Paulo. UN Photo 154,979/Claudio Edinger.

Where available, contraceptive use is growing. Development planning must include education and training of women, with the double aim of enabling women to choose fewer children and of designing more effective rural environmental management strategies. Safer, more convenient and effective birth control methods are needed, among them methods for use by men. Incentives for commercial research in this area are necessary.

The UNFPA (United Nations Population Fund) target is to reduce fertility rates in developing countries from the present level of 3.8 children per woman to 3.3 by the year 2000 and to increase family planning use from 51 percent to 59 percent of the world's families. Meeting this target will be costly. By the end of the century, $9 billion will be needed. Failure to prevent millions upon millions of births will be infinitely more costly for those living now, for the environment, and for governments. India, for example, calculated that population programs prevented 106 million births between 1979 and 1991 and that, at a cost of $7000 to provide education and health care for each child from infancy to adulthood, expenditures totaling $742 billion had been averted.

Governments should continue their growing commitment to stabilizing population growth by supporting UNFPA and other international population agencies. Funding of UNFPA is now at $675 million. Needed is $4.5 billion to reach targets.

Religious leaders can take a stand and educate. It is a painful controversy, not one for the faint of heart, but population growth needs to be discussed in the context of the urgent world crisis.

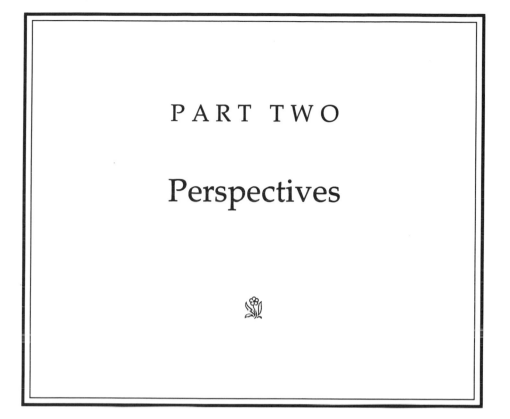

PART TWO

Perspectives

6

THE NEW PROGRESS

SUSAN J. CLARK

WHAT'S WRONG WITH PROGRESS?

We humans are getting better all the time. We are stronger, smarter, and faster than at any time in history, armed with the magic of technology. Living standards, except for the poorest billion of us, have never been so high. We've conquered major diseases; we have more resources and conveniences than our ancestors ever dreamed of having. The achievements of our age are convincing proof that progress is good. We *believe* in progress. We want to "do better" than the last generation did, and that means "having more." This belief gives rise to consumerism, the idea that fulfillment comes from having enough of the right things. The global economy has come to depend on this idea of progress.

The trouble is, we have incurred a horrific cost for this "more each year" dogma. The prosperity we enjoy in the 1990s was gained at the expense of the natural systems that support prosperity — the croplands, grasslands and forests — where nearly all the world's raw materials come from. Raw materials from under the Earth's surface, fossil fuels and minerals, and from the rivers, lakes, and oceans are also threatened by human activity in pursuit of a certain kind of progress.

We are wearing out and using up the Earth systems with mammoth earth-moving machines to build roads and dams and change the course of rivers etched over millennia. Enormous pumps, irrigation systems, and chemicals work the land on every continent in new ways, over time changing the soil's chemistry and causing it to run off the land — 24 billion tons of topsoil is lost every year, totalling one fifth of the world's supply since mid-century. Tremendous industrial plants burn billions of gallons of fossil fuels to power world commerce, breathing enough carbon dioxide into the air to change the chemistry of the global atmosphere. Atmospheric carbon dioxide levels have risen by 13 percent, and the ozone layer has been depleted by 2 percent as a global average. We have crossed critical thresholds, such as the atmosphere's capacity to handle the extra carbon dioxide we send out, and its capacity to shield us from damaging rays of the sun. These things are not *going* to happen, they *have* happened. The crisis is here, and there is very little time in which to act — a few decades at most, scientists estimate.

What looks like the best of economic times, the prosperity of the 1980s and 1990s, is truly an illusion. The world's accounting systems have not yet taken into account the depletion of the resource base. The Gross National Product, GNP, the commonest measure of a nation's prosperity, is a half-century old, and designed neither to reflect the economic impact of a degraded environment, nor the environmental costs of industrial activity, such as global warming. New, more comprehensive and accurate measures are being developed, and they tell a different story.

Progress as we have come to know it is going the way of the dinosaur. The costs are too high — a permanently degraded environment and a billion people living in obscene poverty, facing early death. In addition to its effect on the environment, post–World War II prosperity has also allowed deep inequities among the people of the Earth to grow more entrenched. These inequities are an integral part of the environmental crisis.

INEQUITIES AND PROGRESS

Today's prosperity has been gained at the expense of more than the environment. Vast wealth and power were unevenly distributed even before World War II. Now, the balance of benefits is so far out of proportion that the inequities insult nearly everyone's moral standards and threaten world stability. When an enormous portion of global wealth and power is in the hands of a very few, eventually it can only be held secure by bullying behavior, even force of arms. When moral standards go out the window, can care for the environment and the needs of future generations be far behind?

More wealth went to the industrially developed nations of the North than to the poor nations of the southern hemisphere, more to the already rich than the moderately well off and poor, more to men than to women, more to Americans, Europeans, and Japanese than others. And because this generation is using a disproportionate share of the Earth's resources, more benefits accrue to people living now than to future generations. These morally and politically troubling inequities are now an important part of the crisis of the environment. Global problems have to be solved globally, taking into account everyone's claims to what's left of the global economic pie.

There are agonizing questions. Does the wealth generated by the world's resources belong to everyone, or only to those who contribute the ideas, brain power, sophisticated knowledge, money, and financial risk to produce that wealth? The hours, decades, and lifetimes of work put in by agricultural and industrial workers may have less market value, but how much less? Fourteen million children die of malnutrition and disease every year in developing countries. How do market forces correct for mass starvation?

The impoverishment of Africa, for example, is caused not just by drought and war, but by market forces that are destroying the forests and the fragile safety nets of subsistence agriculture that enabled the people of the Sahel to cope with drought for centuries. Photos of ragged, bony children cannot begin to tell the story of destitute poverty and malnutrition in Africa.

The industrialized nations mine the developing nations for cash at the expense of their resources and their people. To pay interest on crushing debts to northern banks, developing nations produce cash crops such as cotton and coffee on vast tracts of land formerly used to grow food for their own populations. Increasingly urgent demand for cash means more and more land is dedicated to extractive processes such as mining and logging. Degradation of the land is thus a direct result of the debt crisis and inequitable trade policies — factors that are integral to today's prospering global economic order.

The nations of the Third World are set apart and behind by an economic climate that is unfavorable to them; it is the unspoken premise of the present world economic order. The impossible burden of Third World debt results in a net flow of money from the have-nots to the haves. About $50 billion more money is paid yearly by the world's poor to the world's rich, to service the debt, than the poor receive in aid, a morally unacceptable transfer of wealth from poor to rich.

Trade policies disadvantage developing nations and contribute to the downward economic spiral for the South. They include: depressed prices for commodities such as sugar, coffee, and cocoa; protectionism that restricts markets for developing countries' exports; abnormally high interest rates for loans. With their dwindling supplies of cash, nations of the South must import food, water pumps, trucks, and medical supplies at inflated prices, leaving precious little to spend on protecting environmental resources or even basic sanitation services. Developing countries' wealthy elites increasingly invest their money in foreign banks, not at home; such capital flight tightens further the poverty trap so common in the South. Unrealistic military expenditures in Third World nations are encouraged by persuasive vendors, including arms manufacturers and some of their governments, further widening the gap between rich and poor, North and South.

If those who run the great commercial enterprises of the world and their

Environmental activist Wangari Maathai, founder of the Green Belt Movement, Kenya, a tree planting-project run by women, holds a discussion with staff members of the nursery. Photo: UN photo 153,032/Jackie Curtis.

partners, the great political and military enterprises, do not soon supply enough development aid, relief from debt, and fairer trade policies, what will eventually happen? As the rich get richer and the poor multiply their numbers exponentially, will the result be a polarized world of armed enclaves for the rich amid a sea of starvation, wars, and death? In such a scenario, who will care to shoulder the burden of the deteriorating Earth?

If, instead of turning a blind eye to the inequalities and lack of justice that have accompanied the period of greatest economic growth and prosperity the world has ever known, the new progress comes to mean extending the benefits of health and hope to the "bottom billion," and curbing population so it is not the "bottom five billion," then humanity will have a chance to survive in dignity.

Powerful movements are afoot to right these wrongs, rising from the conscience of the people. Strivings for justice are bearing fruit — from the thrust for representative democracy in the former Soviet Union and Eastern Europe, to the proliferation of grassroots movements all over the world.

Groups of women environmental activists are slowly beginning to make a difference in the South. The Chipko Movement in India is dedicated to saving forests. The Greenbelt Movement in Kenya plants millions of trees to save eroding land, to produce firewood, and to earn income. A group of women in Sarawak, Malaysia, protect their way of life by blockading logging routes to prevent the destruction of forests. Women in most of the rural developing world are the de facto managers of the environment because traditional women's work is drawing and hauling water, gathering firewood, and growing, marketing, and cooking the food. In Africa, women grow 70 percent of the food.

Women also hold the reproductive resources of every nation on Earth in their bodies; in this respect at least, they hold the future. Yet they form the vast majority of the world's powerless — the poor and the refugees of the developing world. The environmental consequences of this inequity are wide-ranging and extend into future generations.

Rural Third World women play a vital role in the management of the environment and, with their knowledge and experience, are crucial to achieving sustainable development. With a shift in policies toward correcting the inequities between the sexes and empowering women in the areas of water and land management, access to credit, technology, education and voting rights, nations can better address the mutually reinforcing problems of poverty and resource degradation.

OLD-STYLE PROGRESS:
DRIVEN BY OVERCONSUMPTION

Overconsumption by the world's fortunate is nearly as responsible for the Earth's crisis as are spiraling birth rates. One billion people live in luxury unprecedented in any previous era. Twenty percent of the people consume 80 percent of the Earth's resources. They are the world's consuming class, the car-driving, meat-eating, throwaway society. Support for the affluent lifestyle of the world's wealthiest has been the driving force for damage to the Earth's resource base. Because of overconsumption we have come to the brink of the global economy's limits, and our runaway appetite for consumption threatens to overwhelm even the best efforts to forestall environmental decline.

Since mid-century, the global economic product has quintupled. The world's grain harvest has more than doubled. Large-scale changes like these are depleting the world's natural capital. The farmers of the world cannot expand the food supply much farther. Rice yields have stopped rising. We have exhausted the once-promising green technologies, such as irrigation techniques, chemical inputs, and new seed varieties, and cannot pry very much more grain from the Earth. More land is lost to desertification yearly than is newly planted to crops. Genetic engineering holds promise, but research is expensive and the results are proprietary. Poor nations may not have access to the benefits.

We are already seeing food shortages, despite a record global cereal grain output in 1990. Increases in North America, China, India, and Bangladesh are offset by declining production in Africa and Latin America, resulting in a net increase in the number of countries needing food assistance. Even in this boom year, the world's granaries failed to lay up adequate stores for lean years.

Economists believe the economy is a closed system and that we can all keep helping ourselves to a piece of an ever-expanding pie. But their accounting systems do not yet include a column for a finite store of Earth resources such as fertile soils, rain forests, fossil fuels, and clean air. They have not yet taken into account that there is only one Earth and that the economy is only a subset of the Earth system. A growing economy and an exploding population are not sustainable on this planet.

A dramatic example of how close we are to the Earth's limits is to consider the total land-based photosynthetic product of the Earth. Green plants living on the surface of the Earth take sunlight and a component of the air — carbon dioxide — and turn them into food and other products. This is the source of all the food there will ever be on Earth. The plant cover and its major function — photosynthesis — is a system that has a limit. Humans now use, or have paved over, 40 percent of the Earth's photosynthetic product. With the population expanding and consumption rising, we could double our take to 80 percent of the total available. What other systems would crumble before that could happen is unknown.

Overconsumption, sometimes identified with progress, is a cancerous process that depletes the Earth's resources and widens the gap between rich and poor. Three of the most ecologically important types of consumption are transportation, diet, and use of raw materials.

People who drive cars, 8 percent of all humans, or 400 million people, are directly responsible for 13 percent of all carbon dioxide emissions from fossil fuels. Ninety percent of American new cars have air conditioning, which doubles a car's contribution to climate-changing emissions and adds ozone-depleting CFCs to the atmosphere.

Nearly 40 percent of the world's grain goes to fatten livestock, which is consumed by the meat-eating 25 percent of humanity. American beef is the most extreme example: to produce one pound of beef requires five pounds of grain and the energy equivalent of more than two gallons of gasoline.

Industrial nations and their business firms account for around two-thirds of all use of steel, aluminum, copper, lead, nickel, tin, and zinc, and three-fourths of the energy use. They also produce 99 percent of the world's nuclear warheads, two-thirds of the greenhouse gases responsible for climate change, three-fourths of acid-rain-causing sulfur and nitrogen oxides, 90 percent of ozone-layer-damaging CFCs, and most of the hazardous waste. Americans alone have used up as large a share of the Earth's mineral resources as did everyone who came before them combined. Americans use twenty times as much steel and thirty-five times as much energy as Indians and Indonesians. Consuming classes in developing nations, especially China and India, are growing.

Today's prosperity has been achieved through deficit spending of the limited resources of the Earth. As early as 1973, economist E. F. Schumacher warned of this in *Small Is Beautiful: Economics As If People Mattered*. He wrote:

> A businessman would not consider a firm to have solved its problems of production and to have achieved viability if he saw that it was rapidly consuming its capital. How, then, could we overlook this vital fact when it comes to that very big firm, the economy of Spaceship Earth and, in particular, the economies of its rich passengers?[1]

Futurist and architect Buckminster Fuller saw humankind at a sustainability crossroads in *Operating Manual for Spaceship Earth:*

> In organizing our grand strategy we must first discover where we are now; that is, what our present navigational position in the universal scheme of evolution is. To begin our position-fixing aboard our Spaceship Earth we must first acknowledge that the abundance of immediately consumable, obviously desirable or utterly essential resources has been sufficient until now to allow us to carry on despite our ignorance. Being eventually exhaustible and spoilable, they have been adequate only up to this critical moment. This cushion-for-error of humanity's survival and growth up to now was apparently provided just as a bird inside the egg is provided with liquid nutriment to develop it to a certain point. But then by design the nutriment is exhausted at just the time when the chick is large enough to be able to locomote on its own legs. And so as the chick pecks at the shell seeking more nutriment it inadvertently breaks open the shell. Stepping forth from its initial sanctuary, the young bird must now forage on its own legs and wings to discover the next phase of its regenerative sustenance.
>
> My own picture of humanity today finds us just about to step out from amongst the pieces of our just one-second-ago broken eggshell. Our innocent, trial-and-error-sustaining nutriment is exhausted. We are faced with an entirely new relationship to the universe. We are going to have to spread our wings of intellect and fly or perish; that is, we must dare immediately to fly by the generalized principles governing the universe and not by the ground rules of yesterday's superstitious and erroneously conditioned reflexes. And as we attempt competent thinking we immediately begin to reemploy our innate drive for comprehensive understanding.[2]

---

1. E. F. Schumacher, *Small Is Beautiful: Economics As If People Mattered* (New York: Harper & Row, 1973), 13.

2. Buckminster Fuller, *Operating Manual for Spaceship Earth* (New York: Simon & Schuster, 1970), 51–52.

Humans, from a biologist's point of view, are organisms blindly living as if their environment were unlimited. But we have moved into a new phase of our life cycle on Earth, from a phase in which resources are plentiful to the next in which resources are limited. The human experiment is nearing the carrying capacity of its own environment, and our profligate use of resources is inappropriate to our present phase of life in this great petri dish called Earth, asserts Jeremy Rifkin, in *Entropy: A New World View:*

> The worldwide crisis today is a crisis of transition. In the next age, humanity will have settled into its climactic phase, ordering its activity in such a way as to minimize energy flow-through in the human and social processes. If it doesn't, it will likely go the way of other species who were unable to make the transition in the past. Life's epic is strewn with extinct species; it would have little trouble with accommodating at least one more on the long list of names.[3]

Minimizing energy flow-through means soon replacing our petroleum-based economy with energy alternatives, turning around unsustainable production and consumption patterns and finding new, sustainable ways to serve increasing billions.

STEPS TOWARD A NEW PROGRESS

> A sustainable economy represents nothing less than a higher social order — one as concerned with future generations as with our own, and more focused on the health of the planet and the poor than on material acquisitions and military might. While it is a fundamentally new endeavor, with many uncertainties, it is far less risky than continuing with business as usual.
>
> — Sandra Postel and Christopher Flavin, *Reshaping the Global Economy*

We need to envision immediately a new kind of progress, measured not by economic growth alone, but by the degree to which needs and wants are met without destroying the resource base that belongs to coming generations. Learning to live within the means of the planet will take bold leadership at all levels. Leaders who would apply the golden rule to future generations will insist on using resources sustainably. The new progress would forge a new era of economic activity that is strong, yet socially and environmentally sustainable. To achieve this, people will need new ways of thinking about their lives and their world.

Although economic growth is needed to feed and care for growing populations, to meet development expectations of Third World nations, and to

3. Jeremy Rifkin, in *Entropy: A New World View* (New York: Bantam, 1981).

remedy global environmental problems, industry and agriculture that sub-
tract more from the Earth's natural resource base than they add cannot be
sustained. Economic growth alone has not been able to cure poverty: world
output has quintupled since mid-century, and today more people than ever,
1.2 billion, live in absolute poverty.

Development planners are trying out new measures of prosperity that
use environmental and social indicators — such as reduced pollution and
acidification levels, averted climate change, higher literacy rates, and reduced infant mortality rates — to supplement the Gross National Product
as an index of a nation's economic health.

International cooperation is the top priority. The same concerted effort
that world leaders demonstrate on economic matters is needed now for
the environment. New political and economic models are being forged, for
example, to try to accommodate power struggles between the industrialized
North and the developing South.

Governments can change unsustainable consumption patterns by em-
ploying taxing and pricing policies to make prices reflect the real environmental costs of products. For example, landfill space in perpetuity is part
of the cost of disposable diapers, a cost not reflected in their price. Future
generations will bear some cost in polluted land and water, scarce landfill
space, and possible cleanup costs down the road. Correcting faulty pricing
would use the market system to guide consumers' decisions. Public policy
steps by governments could also favor mass transit over individual car use
and encourage small families over large ones.

Revenues from environmental taxes can be used to pay for domestic
environmental protection and cleanup plans as well as to pay the environmental debt owed to former European colonies in Africa, South Asia, and
Latin America for their part in the unprecedented prosperity now enjoyed in
the North. They could help pay for the training of scientists who will take
integrated rather than traditional single-discipline approaches to the uncertainties inherent in global problems. National and global energy plans
that include renewable energy sources would go a long way to achieving
sustainable progress.

New style leaders can also eliminate environmentally destructive government incentives such as below-cost timber sales, subsidized irrigation
services, and subsidized pesticide use, and replace them with incentives
that reward environmentally sound activity. An example would be to reform
the way utilities are regulated, to encourage efficiency, to decouple profits
from increased sales (California's and New York's plans are examples that
worked), and to tie energy savings to earnings by regulating rates and profits.

•

Third-world/industrialized-world relationships need reform in three broad
areas to help stem the tide of environmental decline: economic development
policies, debt reduction, and trade policies.

Development policies should encourage sustainable use of resources. Strong programs are needed to pursue agricultural reforms and directly alleviate poverty instead of continuing to mount large-scale infrastructure and industrial projects of often dubious value, such as dams and factories, that rely on the now discredited trickle-down theory of development. The transfer of sustainable energy technologies to the Third World is important if we are to avert large-scale increases in global warming and pollution as these nations develop industrially. Lending and aid practices must be guided by a vision of a sustainable global economy.

Northern industrial nations and banks are looking for ways to reduce Third World debt, by writing down some loans and forgiving some. Debt reduction plans that are conditional on the receiving nation taking steps to protect its environment, although unpopular in the South, are probably necessary.

If richer nations would promote trade policies that have positive effects on the global environment, perhaps they could slow the fall by Third World economies into disastrous economic collapse. They might allow countries to set trade restrictions that protect their resource base and environment, such as the import ban on African ivory and the bans on raw log exports set by Indonesia and Thailand. They would do well to discourage attempts to "harmonize" environmental policies as part of general trade agreements, which have the effect of reducing all nations to the lowest common denominator of environmental safety.

For individuals, taming the dragon of overconsumption will take a shift in the way we see things. First, we can hope to replace the passion for possessions with more meaningful measures of well-being. As central sources of fulfillment, intangibles that enrich the heart, spirit, and mind are better for the Earth.

Second, we can gradually shift some basic perceptions about consumption. One way is to see greed differently. Greed is nothing new, but what is new is how much damage it can do to the Earth, wreaking more havoc per person because technology allows it. Perhaps the sea of advertising messages worldwide, equating consumption with happiness, would come to be seen critically. Then, hopefully, shopping as a cultural activity by the wealthy of the world would lose favor, and the commercial market would lose much of its power to invade and manipulate private life.

Equating consumption with personal fulfillment might come to be seen as a disease state from which we are beginning to recover. The compulsion to consume may come to be seen the same way cigarette smoking is now seen: a harmful, outdated addiction. The vaccine of environmental awareness and common sense may soon be strong enough to give people immunity to consumerism.

7

THE SPIRITUALITY
OF THE EARTH

THOMAS BERRY

The subject we are concerned with is the spirituality of the Earth. By this I do not mean a spirituality that is directed toward an appreciation of the Earth. I speak of the Earth as subject, not as object. I am concerned with the maternal principle out of which we were born and whence we derive all that we are and all that we have. In our totality we are born of the Earth. We are earthlings. The Earth is our origin, our nourishment, our support, our guide. Our spirituality itself is Earth-derived. If there is no spirituality in the Earth, then there is no spirituality in ourselves. The human and the Earth are totally implicated in the other.

Not to recognize the spirituality of the Earth is to indicate a radical lack of spiritual perception in ourselves. We see this lack of spiritual insight in the earlier attitude of Euro-Americans in their inability to perceive the spiritual qualities of the indigenous American peoples and their mysticism of the land. The attack on these spiritual qualities by Christians constitutes one of the most barbaric moments in Christian history. This barbarism turned upon the tribal peoples was loosed also upon the American earth with a destructive impact beyond calculation.

Historian Thomas Berry is one of the world's most respected environmental theologians. A Passionist priest, born in 1914 in North Carolina, Berry's *Dream of the Earth* and his earlier *Riverdale Papers* are classics in the field. He founded the Riverdale Center for Religious Research in Riverdale, New York, where he now devotes his time to the study of the role of humans in the dynamics of the planet Earth and the universe.

The fragility of the Earth has not yet impressed itself upon us. The crassness of our relation to the Earth cannot but indicate a radical absence of spirituality in ourselves, not the lack of a spiritual dimension of the Earth. The opaqueness is in our understanding of the Earth, not in the Earth's structure, which expresses an abiding numinous presence. The Earth process has been generally ignored by the religious-spiritual currents of the West. Our alienation goes so deep that it is beyond our conscious mode of awareness. While there are tributes to the Earth in the scriptures and in Christian liturgy, there is a tendency to see the Earth as a seductive reality that brought about alienation from God in the agricultural peoples of the Near East. Earth worship was the ultimate idolatry, the cause of the Fall, and thereby the cause of sacrificial redemption by divine personality. Thus, too, the Christian sense of being crucified to the world and living only for the savior. This personal savior orientation has led to an interpersonal devotionalism that quite easily dispenses with Earth except as a convenient support for life.

We can produce Christian spiritualities that function in a certain isolated context without regard for the larger society. But such redemptive spiritualities are not liable to be effective in our secular world. It speaks a rhetoric that is not available for our secular world, or, if it is available, it widens rather than lessens the tragic inner division between the world of affairs and the world of divine communion. It does not offer a way of interpreting the inner life of the society itself in a rhetoric available to the society. It does not establish an understanding of that authentic experience in contemporary life which is oriented toward communion with creation processes. Indeed, it does not recognize that the context of any authentic spirituality lies in the creation myth that governs the total life orientation.

Creation in traditional Christian teaching is generally presented as part of the tract on "God in himself and in relation to his creation." But creation in this metaphysical, biblical, medieval, theological context is not terribly helpful in understanding the creation process as this is set forth in the scientific manuals or the textbooks of Earth science, of life sciences such as they are studied by children in elementary and high school, or later in college.

These classroom studies initiate the child into a world that has more continuity with later adult life in its functional aspect than does the catechetical story of creation taken from biblical sources. This schoolroom presentation of the world in which the child lives and finds a place is all important for the future spirituality of the child. The school fulfills in our times the role of the ancient initiation rituals which introduced our children to the society and to their human and sacred roles in this society. The tragedy is that the sacred or spiritual aspect of the initiation process is now absent. The child is given a physical process, a marvelous story of the emergence of the universe, of the Earth and of the human, but without reference to the spiritual aspect of this process. It is doubtful if separate catechetical instructions with their heavy emphasis on redemptive processes can ever supply what is missing.

It may be that the later alienation of young adults from the redemptive sacramental tradition is, in some degree, due to this inability to communicate to the child a spirituality grounded more deeply in universe dynamics in accord with the modern way of experiencing the galactic emergence of the universe, the shaping of the Earth, the appearance of life, of human consciousness, and the historical sequence in human development.

In this sequence the child might learn that the Earth has its intrinsic spiritual quality from the beginning, for this aspect of the creation story is what has been missing. This is what needs to be established if we are to have a functional spirituality. Just how to give the child an integral world, that is the issue. It is also the spiritual issue of the modern religious personality. Among our most immediate tasks is to establish this new sense of the Earth and of the human as a function of the Earth.

We need to understand that the Earth acts in all that acts upon the Earth. The Earth acts in us whenever we act. In and through the Earth, spiritual energy is present. This spiritual energy emerges in the total complex of Earth functions. Each form of life is integrated with every other life form. Even beyond the Earth, by force of gravitation, every particle of the physical world attracts and is attracted to every other particle. This attraction holds the differentiated universe together and enables it to be a universe of individual realities. The universe is not a vast smudge of matter, some jelly-like substance extended indefinitely in space. Nor is the universe a collection of unrelated particles. The universe is, rather, a vast multiplicity of individual realities with both qualitative and quantitative differences all in spiritual physical communion with each other. The individuals of similar form are bound together in their unity of form. The species are related to each other by derivation: the later, more complex forms are derived from earlier, more simple life forms.

The first shaping of the universe was into those great galactic systems of fiery energy that constitute the starry heavens. In these celestial furnaces the elements are shaped. Eventually, after some ten billion years, the solar system and the Earth are born out of the stardust resulting from exploded stars. Earth, particularly, is our concern. So far as we know, Earth and its living forms constitute a unique planet in the entire complex of the universe. Here on Earth, life, both plant and animal life, was born in the primordial seas some three billion years ago. Plants came upon the land some six hundred million years ago after the planet Earth had shaped itself through a great series of transformations in forming the continents, the mountains, the valleys, the rivers and streams. The atmosphere was long in developing. The animals came ashore a brief interval later. As these life forms established themselves over some hundreds of millions of years, the luxuriant foliage formed layer after layer of organic matter which was then buried in the crust of the Earth to become fossil formations with enormous amounts of stored energy. One hundred million years ago flowers appeared and the full beauty of Earth began to manifest itself. Some sixty million years ago the birds were in the air. Mammals walked through the forest. Some of the mammals, the whales and the porpoises and dolphins, went back into the sea.

Finally some two million years ago, the ascending forms of life culminated in the awakening consciousness of man. Wandering food gatherers and hunters until some eight thousand years ago, we then settled into village life. This led through the neolithic period to the classical civilization which has flourished so brilliantly for the past five thousand years.

Then, some four hundred years ago, a new stage of scientific development took place which, in the eighteenth and nineteenth centuries, brought about a human technological dominance of the Earth out of which we had emerged. This can be interpreted as the Earth awakening to consciousness itself in its human mode of being. The story of this awakening consciousness is the most dramatic aspect of the Earth story.

The spiritual attitude that then caused or permitted humans to attack the Earth with such savagery as we witness has never been adequately explained. That it was done by a Christian-derived society, and even with the belief that this was the truly human and Christian task, makes explanation especially harsh for our society.

Possibly it was the millennial drives toward a total transformation of the Earth condition that led us, resentful that the perfect world was not yet achieved by divine means, to set about the violent subjugating of the Earth by our own powers in the hope that in this way the higher life would be attained, our afflictions healed.

While this is the positive goal sought it must be added that the negative, even fearful, attitude toward the Earth resulting from the general hardships of life led to the radical disturbance of the entire Earth process. The increasing intensity shown in exploiting the Earth was also the result of the ever-rising and unsatiated expectation of Western peoples. Even further, the natural antagonisms of Earth were fostered by the Darwinian principle of natural selection, indicating that the primary attitude of each individual and each species is for its own survival at the expense of the others. Out of this strife, supposedly, the glorious achievements of Earth take place. Darwin had only minimal awareness of the cooperative and mutual dependence of each form of life on the other forms of life. This is amazing since he himself discovered the great web of life. Still, he had no real appreciation of the principle of inter-communion.

Much more needs to be said on the conditions that permitted such a mutually destructive situation to arise between ourselves and the Earth, but we must pass on to give some indication of the new attitude that needs to be adopted toward the Earth. This involves a new spiritual and even mystical communion with the Earth, a true aesthetic of the Earth, a sensitivity to Earth needs, a valid economy of the Earth. We need a way of designating the Earth-human world in its continuity and identity rather than in its discontinuity and difference. In spirituality, especially, we need to recognize the numinous qualities of the Earth. We might begin with some awareness of what it is to be human, what is the role of consciousness on the Earth, the place of the human species in the universe.

While the scholastic definition of the human as a rational animal gives us some idea of ourselves among the biological species, it gives us a rather inadequate sense of the role we play in the total Earth process. The Chinese have a better definition of the human as the *hsin* of heaven and Earth. This word *hsin* is written as a pictograph of the human heart. It should be translated by a single word or a phrase with both a feeling and an understanding aspect. It could be thus translated by saying that the human is the "understanding heart of heaven and Earth." Even more briefly, the phrase has been translated by Julia Ch'ing in the statement that the human is "the heart of the universe." Here we have a remarkable feeling for the absolute dimensions of the human, the total integration of reality in the human, the total integration of the human within the reality of things.

We need a spirituality that emerges out of a reality deeper than ourselves, even deeper than life, a spirituality that is as deep as the Earth process itself, a spirituality that is born out of the solar system. There in the stars is where the primordial elements take shape in both their physical and psychic aspects. Out of these elements the solar system and the Earth took shape, and out of the Earth, ourselves.

There is a certain triviality in any spiritual discipline that does not experience itself as supported by the spiritual as well as the physical dynamics of the entire cosmic-Earth process. Spirituality is a mode of being in which not only the divine and the human commune with each other, but in which we discover ourselves in the universe and the universe discovers itself in us. The Sioux Indian Crazy Horse called upon these depths of his own being when he invoked the cosmic forces to support himself in battle. He painted lightning upon his cheek, placed a rock behind his ear, an eagle feather in his hair, and the head of a hawk upon his head. Assumption of the cosmic insignia is also evident in the Sun Dance Ceremony. In this dance the symbols of the sun and moon and stars are cut out of rawhide and worn by the dancers. The world of living, moving things is indicated by the form of the buffalo cut from rawhide, and by the eagle feathers. The plant world is represented by the cottonwood tree set up in the center of the ceremonial circle. The supreme spirit itself is represented by the circular form of the dance area.

So the spiritual personality should feel constantly in communion with those numinous cosmic forces out of which we were born. This cosmic-Earth order needs to be supplemented by the entire historical order of human development such as was depicted on the shield of Aeneas by Virgil. Virgil spends several long pages enumerating the past and future historical events wrought on the shield of Aeneas. All these forces are presently available to us in a new mode of appreciation. The historical and the cosmic can be seen as a single process. This vision of Earth-human development provides the sustaining dynamic of the contemporary world.

That there is an organizing force within the Earth process with both physical and psychic dimensions needs to be acknowledged in language and in imagery. It needs to be named and spoken of in its integral form. It has a unified functioning similar to the more particular organisms with which we are acquainted. When we speak of Earth we are speaking of a numinous maternal principle in and through which the total complex of Earth phenomena takes its shape.

In antiquity this mode of being of the Earth was indicated by personification. The "Earth" itself designates a deity in Hesiod and in the Homeric hymns. This personification is expressed as Cybele in the Eastern Mediterranean and as Demeter in the Greek world. Biblical revelation represents a basic antagonism between the transcendent deity, Jahweh, and the fertility religions of the surrounding societies. There is a basic effort here to keep the asymmetry in the relationship between the divine and the created. In the doctrine of the Madonna in later Christian history there are many passages indicating that Mary was to be thought of as the Earth in which the True Vine is planted and which had been made fruitful by the Holy Spirit. This Mary-Earth equation was not as adequately developed as it might have been in association with the doctrine of the Incarnation.

Probably it belongs to the dialectics of history that the first direct human association with these unique historical individuals, the savior and his mother, has to develop before any adequate feeling for the mystique of the Earth could take place. Perhaps, too, a full development of redemption processes was needed before this new mode of human-Earth communion could find expression in our times.

However this may be, a shift in attention is now taking place. Several things are happening. The most notable single event is that modern science is giving us a new and more comprehensive account of our own birth out of the Earth. This story of the birth of the human was never known so well as now. After discovery of the geological stages of Earth transformation and the discovery of the sequence of life in ancient fossil remains by Louis le Clerc, James Hutton, and Charles Lyell, then came the discovery of the emergence of all forms of life from primordial life forms by Charles Darwin, presented in his *Origin of Species* in 1859. While Darwin saw the human appearance only out of the physical Earth, Teilhard de Chardin saw the human emerging out of both the physical and the psychic dimensions of the Earth. Thus the whole burden of modern Earth studies is to narrate the story of the birth of the human from our Mother the Earth.

Once this story is told, it immediately becomes obvious how significant the title Mother Earth really is, how intimate a relationship exists, how absolute our gratitude must be, how delicate our concern. Our long motherless period is coming to a close. Hopefully, too, the long period of our mistreatment of Earth is being terminated. If it is not terminated, if we fail to perceive not only our Earth origin but also our continuing dependence on our Earth-mother, then it will be due in no small measure to the ephemeral spiritualities that have governed our own thoughts and attitudes and actions.

In this mother-child relationship, however, a new and fundamental shift in dependence has now taken place. Until recently, the child was taken care of by the mother. Now, however, the mother must be extensively cared for by the child. The child has grown to adult status. The mother-child relationship needs to undergo a renewal similar to that in the ordinary process of maturing. In this process both child and mother experience a period of alienation. Then follows a reconciliation period when mother and child relate to each other with a new type of intimacy, a new depth of appreciation, and a new mode of interdependence. Such is the historical period in which we are now living. Development of this new mode of Earth-human communion can only take place within a profound spiritual context. Thus the need for a spirituality that will encompass this process.

As a second observation concerning our newly awakening sense of the Earth, we could say that a new phase in the history of the madonna figure of Western civilization has begun. Association of the Virgin Mother with the Earth may now be a condition of Mary returning to her traditional role in Western civilization. Her presence may also be a condition for overcoming our estrangement from the Earth. In the Western world the Earth known only in itself as universal mother is not sufficient. It must be identified with a historical person in and through whom Earth functions in its ultimate reaches. Phrases referring to Mary as the Earth are found throughout Western religious literature. Whether this is anything more than a simple rhetorical device needs a thorough inquiry at the present time. But whether or not this relationship is given in any extensive manner in prior Christian literature, it is a subject of utmost importance for our entire civilizational venture. Few, if any, other civilizations were so deeply grounded in a feminine mystique as the medieval period of Western Christendom. A vital contact with this earlier phase of Western civilization is hardly possible without some deep appreciation of its feminine component. Thus we cannot fail to unite in some manner these two realities: Earth and Mary. The Earth needs embodiment in a historical person, and such a historical person needs an Earth identity to fulfill adequately her role as divine mother.

A third observation is that emergence of the new age of human culture will necessarily be an age dominated by the symbol of woman. This, too, depends on the identification of woman with the Earth and its creativity. Woman and Earth, these two are inseparable. The fate of one is the fate of the other. This association is given in such a variety of cultural developments throughout the world in differing historical periods that it is hardly possible to disassociate these two. Earth consciousness, woman consciousness: these two go together. Both play a stupendous role in the spirituality of the human as well as in the structure of civilizations. Our alienation from the Earth, from ourselves, and from a truly creative man-woman relationship in an overly masculine mode of being demands a reciprocal historical period in which not only a balance will be achieved but even, perhaps, a period of feminine emphasis.

A fourth observation I would make is to note our new capacity for subjectivity, for subjective communion with the manifold presences that constitute the universe. In this we are recovering the more primitive genius of humankind. For in our earlier years we experienced both the intimacy and the distance of our relation with the Earth and with the entire natural world. Above all we lived in a spirit world, a world that could be addressed in a reciprocal mood of affectionate concern. This is what gave rise to sympathetic magic as well as to the great rituals, the majestic poetry, and the awesome architecture of past ages. Nothing on Earth was a mere "thing." Every being had its own divine, numinous subjectivity, its self, its center, its unique identity. Every being was a presence to every other being. Among the more massive civilizations, China gave clearest expression to this intimacy of beings with each other in its splendid concept of *Jen*, a word that requires translation according to context by a long list of terms in English, terms such as love, goodness, human-heartedness, affection. All beings are held together in *Jen*, as in St. Paul all things are held together in Christ. But perhaps an even better analogy is to say that while for Newton, the universal law of gravitation whereby each particle of matter in the universe indicates a mere physical force of attraction, the universal law of attraction for the Chinese is a form of feeling identity.

For this reason there is, in China, the universal law of compassion. This is especially observable in humankind, for every human has a heart that cannot bear to witness the suffering of others. When objection was made to Wang Yang-ming in the fifteenth century that this is evident only in human relations, Master Wang replied by noting that even the frightened cry of the bird, or the crushing of a plant, or the shattering of a tile, or the senseless breaking of a stone immediately and spontaneously causes pain in the human heart. This would not be, he tells us, unless there exists a bond of intimacy and even identity between ourselves and these other beings.

Recovery of this capacity for subjective communion with the Earth is a consequence and a cause of a newly-emerging spirituality. Subjective communion with the Earth, identification with the cosmic-Earth-human process, provides the context in which we now make our spiritual journey. This journey is no longer the journey of Dante through the heavenly spheres. It is no longer simply the journey of the Christian community through history to the heavenly Jerusalem. It is the journey of primordial matter through its marvelous sequence of transformations, in the stars, in the Earth, in living beings, in human consciousness toward an ever more complete spiritual-physical intercommunion of the parts with each other, with the whole, and with that numinous presence which has ever been manifested throughout this entire cosmic-Earth-human process.

8

DOING THEOLOGY
ON A SMALL PLANET

TIMOTHY WEISKEL

But man, proud man,
Drest in a little brief authority,
Most ignorant of what he's most assur'd,
His glassy essence, like an angry ape,
Plays such fantastic tricks before high heaven,
As make the angels weep ...

— Shakespeare

OUR CIRCUMSTANCE

We live on the third planet from the sun, our closest star. As stars go, it is not a very big one. Nor is the planet, for that matter. Even with gadgets of our own making, it can be circled in an hour or so. It's a pretty small place to call home in the vastness of all that we have come to know as creation.

Yet home it is, and an extremely vulnerable one at that. Most of the planet is covered with water, some of which periodically turns to ice in

Timothy Weiskel, an ecological anthropologist and historian, has taught at Williams College, Harvard, and Yale. He earned his B.A. at Yale and his doctorate at Oxford University as a Rhodes Scholar. His publications include studies on history, anthropology, and ecology of West Africa, as well as environmental ethics. He is currently director of the Harvard Seminar on Environmental Values at Harvard Divinity School.

the high latitudes as solar radiation and the planet's orbital trajectory vary over time. Moreover, the planet is enclosed in an improbable envelope of gases whose precise proportions — essential for our existence — can only be maintained through the continuous metabolism of countless life-forms on or near its surface. Species, populations, and communities of these life-forms co-evolve over time in response to the alternate rhythms of ice and warmth and the variation of habitat created by drifting continental plates, changing sea levels, and shifting regional climates.

Humans are a recent arrival in the community of life-forms, prospering during the inter-glacial period only over the past million years of a three-billion-year continuum — that is, in roughly the last 0.03 percent of life's unfolding drama. Moreover, it now seems probable that we will not endure any longer than many of the other transient life-forms that have left traces of their bones or behavior in the sands and sediments of time. The capacity for intelligence which humans possess may not prove to be an adaptive trait in the long run, especially since human intelligence is frequently deployed to kill fellow humans or extinguish other life-supporting organisms crucial for long-term human survival.

In biological terms humans provide no essential functions for the survival of other large communities of life forms — save, perhaps, for our own domesticated animals, plants and parasites. If we disappear it is probable that wheat, rice, cattle, camels, and the common cold virus will not survive in their current forms for very long. But the vast majority of the Earth's organisms can do perfectly well, indeed perhaps thrive even better, without us or our biological associates.

OUR BELIEFS

None of this is news. Common sense and a junior high school education can impress this much upon our minds. Yet the curious fact is that we refuse to believe it. We continue to strut and prance about with a sense of supreme self-importance as if all creation were put in place for our benefit. As the zoologist David Ehrenfeld has observed, in spite of what science has revealed about our place in the universe "we still believe that the force of gravity exists in order to make it easier for us to sit down."

From where does such arrogance come? How can our beliefs be so far out of touch with our knowledge? How can we maintain such an inflated sense of personal, collective, and species self-importance?

The answer, in part, is that Western religious traditions have generated and sustained this petty arrogance. A culture's religious beliefs are constructed from what that group has come to believe in religiously. Ever since the advent of cereal agriculture and with increasing intensity since the emergence of humanist thought stemming from the European renaissance, Western cultures have come to believe religiously in their own power, importance, and capacity to dominate and control nature.

Some religious groups have transcribed and elaborated creation myths which serve to ennoble and authorize this illusion of domination. In these myths a supreme and omnipotent god figure (usually portrayed as male) is said to have created humankind and enjoined this species to be "fruitful and multiply" and "subdue" the Earth. Moreover, these traditions often feature selected human groups who come to feel entitled and empowered or specially ordained by such a god to be his "chosen people." Through their actions and history, it is believed, this god allegedly manifested his intent for the planet as a whole. In short, human groups created "God" in their own image and generated divine narratives that accorded themselves privileged status in the whole of creation.

If the monumental arrogance of such belief systems seems parochial and silly in our day, they are nonetheless understandable in the historical context in which they emerged. For well over 90 percent of human history, of course, the notion of humans conquering or subduing nature was patently absurd. As a foraging species, humankind could only survive by developing a complex understanding of mutual respect and reciprocity with a broad range of other life-forms. We know little of their religious beliefs, but among human communities prior to sedentary agriculture there is little evidence of belief in human dominance over nature.

With the advent of urban-organized cereal agriculture, however, the illusion of human control over nature appeared at least partially plausible and rapidly became widespread. Selective plant breeding, animal domestication, and irrigation technology made it possible to capture large volumes of solar energy and accumulate multi-annual foodstuff surpluses. Simultaneously, the heightened ecological vulnerability of agro-ecosystems and the appearance of new forms of virulent disease caused sporadic crop blight and disease epidemics. These phenomena, in turn, made surplus foodstuff accumulation an absolute necessity for the continued survival of villages, towns, and cities. Access to arable land and a tractable labor force constituted the only assurance of continuous surplus, and the control of both these elements of production became the object of organized social activity. Competition for land and labor often took the form of open conflict and warfare, leading to the development of ideas systems that valued conquest and subordination and inscribed these metaphors in the underlying belief structure in agricultural communities. Hierarchy, power, control, and domination were all real-life experiences for agricultural peoples locked in the struggle to control land and labor. It is, thus, hardly surprising that these metaphors came to characterize the beliefs that these communities held to religiously in an attempt to understand their world and conceptualize their position within it.

The illusion of control over nature received further emphatic support in recent Western history from the experience of European overseas expansion since the Renaissance. In the brief period of a few centuries, European peoples expanded upon vast and thinly peopled regions of the world, carrying with them their crops, animals, weeds, pests, and diseases. These associated "biological allies" devastated native flora, fauna, and human populations in large portions of the world, and western Europeans succeeded in establishing "neo-Europes" in regions of North and South America, Australia, New Zealand, and South Africa. As "white settler" societies, these groups often perceived themselves as "frontier societies," for it was along the frontiers of interaction with native species that these cultures experienced their self-defining moments of successful domination.

Perhaps even more important, the history of this expansion has led Western cultures and the Westernized elites in Third World countries to believe in the illusion of unlimited growth. The industrial revolution and discovery of fossil energy sources further sustained the belief in infinite growth. Having expanded upon the things of nature, modern humankind has come to believe that expansion is in the nature of things. This is not so, of course, but we are only now just beginning to discover that this cherished belief is potentially fatal illusion.

OUR TASK

We need to change our habits of mind and action in the very near future. Furthermore, this promises to be a struggle. Abandoning the belief in growth will be difficult enough in the Western world, but it is likely to be even more difficult in the Third World because the dream of an expanding economy seems to be all that political leaders currently have to hold out as hopeful for the burgeoning populations of these regions. Any serious effort to question the economics of perpetual growth raises the ugly and disconcerting question of resource distribution and consumption. Political leaders are reluctant to address this embarrassing issue and prefer to stoke the fires of expanding Third World economic growth instead of designing durable systems of steady-state economics.

Mounting evidence concerning the role of humans in natural ecosystems indicates that the world ecosystem cannot long endure a widescale replication of the resource-depleting patterns of recent Western growth. Indeed, the science of ecology is suggesting that many of our religiously held beliefs — like the belief in perpetual economic growth — are in fact colossal illusions. We cannot meaningfully subdue nature for very long. There are no permanent frontiers in an ecosystem. Unrestrained growth on a small planet is simply not possible. Human domination of nature is a paradox, for our "control" of nature can only be achieved by understanding its laws and subordinating ourselves to them.

Most of our received theological formulations are pitifully out of touch with this current ecological understanding. In fact many religious leaders, like many politicians, actively resist the insights of ecology, for these ideas entail a fundamental reformulation of both public policy and humanist belief in our contemporary world. Clearly there is much work for theologians to undertake in re-examining the received tradition.

Yet even more than this will be needed because science itself has become the cornerstone of modern humankind's religiously held belief in human control. In our era, this kind of arrogant science, like the self-important religious traditions of the past, must be questioned by a new ecumenical theology of creation and a realistic understanding of human agency. If we are going to survive as a species, we need now to develop a radical sense of humility and subordination to a re-sanctified and holy nature. Nevertheless, because modern science and technology often engender and sustain the powerful illusion of control, we are in danger — as Shakespeare observed — of being most ignorant of what we are most assured.

Political leaders are equally guilty of the arrogant illusions that have characterized religious traditions and scientific endeavors alike. "Drest in a little brief authority," elected politicians have come to think that they are in charge of the world. In the public policy they formulate they play fantastic tricks with the world's resources for the reputed benefit of groups that elected them. But what of those who cannot vote for parliamentarians? What of future human generations? What about other species? It is no wonder that angels weep.

The time has come for contemporary theologians to re-state some simple truths: we did not create the world; we cannot control it. Instead, we must learn in full humility to live with all other creatures within its limits. As it was once made clear to Job, it is not by *our* wisdom that the hawk soars and spreads its wings toward the south. Indeed, we are only beginning to discover the precious intricacy and fragility of the life webs laid down billions of years before we appeared. Realization of these simple truths could lead to a fundamental reformulation of public policy and our collective beliefs, both of which will be required for our survival as a species. Scientists, politicians, and religious communities alike sorely need what theologians must now provide — a positive vocabulary of human limit in a sanctified and sustainable creation. In short, we all stand in need of a theology for a small planet.

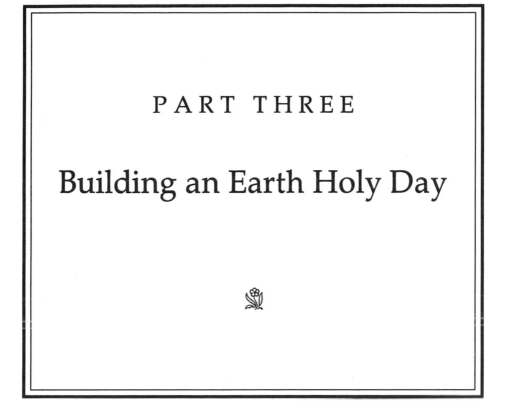

PART THREE

Building an Earth Holy Day

9

THE ASSISI
RELIGION AND NATURE
INTERFAITH CEREMONY

Following is an adaptation of the liturgies used on September 29, 1986, for a ceremony in the Basilica of St. Francis, Assisi, Italy. This ceremony was originally designed by an international liturgy working party at the request of the World Wildlife Foundation International, for the celebration of its twenty-fifth anniversary. Five faiths were represented: Buddhism, Christianity, Hinduism, Islam, and Judaism. The ceremony originally consisted of five separate liturgies running in parallel, with highlights from each shared in common.

ASSEMBLY AND PROCESSION

Behold! In the creation of the heavens and the earth
and in the alternation of the night and day
are signs of understanding for humankind.

Such as remember God standing, sitting, and reclining,
and ponder the creation of the heavens and the earth, and say:
Yours is the Glory.
Preserve us from the doom of Fire!"

— From the Qur'an, Surah III: 190–191.

CREATION AND NATURE

This section rejoices in creation and nature through poetry and songs in praise of the Earth.

Let Heaven Praise the Lord

Alleluia!

Let heaven praise the Lord:
praise him, heavenly heights,
praise him, all his angels,
praise him, all his armies!

Praise him, sun and moon,
praise him, shining stars,
praise him, highest heavens,
and waters above the heavens!

Let them all praise the name of the Lord
at whose command they were created;
he has fixed them in their place for ever,
by an unalterable statute.

Let earth praise the Lord:
sea-monsters and all the deeps,
fire and hail, snow and mist,
gales that obey his decree,

mountains and hills,
orchards and forests,
wild animals and farm animals,
snakes and birds,

all kings on earth and nations,
princes, all rulers in the world,
young men and girls,
old people, and children too!

Let them all praise the name of the Lord,
for his name and no other is sublime,
transcending earth and heaven in majesty,
raising the fortunes of his people,
to the praises of the devout,
of Israel, the people dear to him.

Alleluia.

                — The Holy Bible, Psalm 148

There Was at First

There was at first no Being. . . .

There was no air, nor sky beyond.
What was in it? Where?
In whose protection?
Was water there, deep beyond measure?

There was no death, nor deathless state,
no night, no day.
The One breathed, without breath
by its own power.
There was nothing else: no, nothing else.

Darkness lay wrapped in darkness.
All was water, all, all over.
Love began, at first; desire
was the seed of mind.

Sages and poets, searching within,
saw the link of Being in non-Being.
But who really knows? Who can tell —
How it was born, where creation began?
The gods came later: Who then knows
That from which creation came,
Whether founded well or not?

He who sees from heaven above,
He only knows. Or, He too knows it not!

A Hindu song of creation, based upon the Creation Veda

REPENTANCE

We have all failed to care for nature. We all need to start afresh. The traditional Jewish call to repentance is made by the blowing of the shofar, or the ram's horn. It is sounded in all four directions, to call the whole world to repentance for its failure to care.

Homage to the Three Jewels: Song of the Prayer of Truth

You, the Sugatas (Those Gone to Bliss) of the three times,
and your spiritual sons and their disciples,
who possess a great ocean-like wealth of infinite good qualities,
and who regard all powerless migrating beings as your only sons;
please listen attentively to my true words of sorrow.

May those actions,
the ten aspects of Dharma practice,
of scholars and accomplished ones who hold dearly
the complete Dharma of the Able one (the Buddha),
that dispels the sufferings of cyclic existence and (solitary) peace
and that flourishes in this vast world
as a wealth of happiness and benefit,
increase forevermore.

Please pacify the uninterrupted miseries and unbearable fears,
such as famines and sicknesses,
that torment powerless beings
completely oppressed by inexhaustible and violent evils,
and henceforth lead us from suffering states
and place us in an ocean of happiness and joy.

Those who, maddened by the demons of delusion,
commit violent negative actions
that destroy both themselves and others,
should be the objects of our compassion.
May the hosts of undisciplined beings
fully gain the eye that knows
what to abandon and practice,
and be granted a wealth
of loving-kindness and friendliness.

Through the force of dependent-arising,
which by nature is profound
and empty of appearances,
the force of the Words of Truth,
the power of the kindness of the Three Jewels
and the true power of non-deceptive actions and their effects;
may my prayer of truth be accomplished quickly without hindrance.

— His Holiness the XIVth Dalai Lama

The Hindu Call to Repentance

You are the Father of the universe,
whatever is moving and unmoving.
You are the great Teacher,
who is to be worshipped by humankind.
O Lord of unequalled power,
none exists that is equal to you in the triple universe;
how then can there be anyone superior?

Hundreds of pilgrims stream toward the Basilica of St. Francis, where Prince Philip and the five religious representatives wait to receive banners from the pilgrimage leaders. The pilgrims walked along four different routes across the Umbrian countryside, converging on Assisi to participate in the Interfaith Ceremony. Photo: Claude Berger.

Therefore, bowing down and prostrating my body before you,
O adorable Lord,
I crave your forgiveness.
As a father to his devoted son,
as a friend to his dear friend,
as a lover to his beloved,
even so, O Lord, shouldst thou bear with me.

— From the Bhagavad-Gita, XI 43–44

CELEBRATION

In this section we formally and symbolically show our need for one another in caring for nature. At the start of the section, a procession brings rakshas, or ribbons for the wrist, to the center stage. The procession can include representatives of different faiths and environmental groups.

The tying on of rakshas is a Hindu custom that takes place at the festival of Raksha Bandan, when sisters tie bracelets onto the arms of the man in the family who protects them, saying "while you protect me physically, I protect you spiritually." It expresses the need of one for the other. At the Assisi ceremony, His Royal Highness the Duke of Edinburgh said, "When you tie a raksha onto your neighbor's wrist, and receive one in return, you are expressing the message that the conservation of nature depends on the cooperation of all people, and that it can only be achieved by a combination of practical measures and emotional commitment."

Banners for each faith and environmental group may be brought forward at this time, to prepare for the Sending Forth. All stand for the procession, then take seats.

There Is No Difference

These Buddhist verses express the attitude that lies at the heart of a Bodhisattva, one who aspires to attain enlightenment for the welfare of others. The Bodhisattva realizes that all suffering, from the personal to the global, arises from self-concern.

As no one desires the slightest suffering
nor ever has enough of happiness,
there is no difference between myself and others,
so let me make others joyfully happy.

May all beings everywhere
plagued with sufferings of body and mind
obtain an ocean of happiness and joy
by virtue of my merits.

May those feeble with cold find warmth,
and may those oppressed with heat be cooled
by the boundless waters that pour forth
from the great clouds of the Bodhisattvas (merits).

May the regions of desolation become places of joy
with vast and fragrant lotus pools
beautified with the exquisite calls
of wild ducks, geese, and swans.

May the rains of lava, blazing stones and weapons
from now on become a rain of flowers,
and may all battling with weapons
from now on be a playful exchange of flowers.

May all animals be free from the fear
of being eaten by one another;
may the hungry ghosts be as happy
as men of Lands of Plenty.

May the naked find clothing,
the hungry find food;
may the thirsty find water
and delicious drinks.

May the frightened cease to be afraid
and those bound be freed;
may the powerless find power,
and may people think of benefiting one another.

For as long as space endures
and for as long as living beings remain,
until then may I too abide
to dispel the misery of the world.

May all the pains of living creatures
ripen (solely) upon myself,
and through the might of the Bodhisattva Sangha
may all beings experience happiness.

May all embodied creatures
uninterruptedly hear
the sound of Dharma issuing from birds and trees,
beams of light and even space itself.

May there abound in all directions
gardens of wish-fulfilling trees
filled with the sweet sound of Dharma
proclaimed by the Buddhas and the Bodhisattvas.

— From Shantideva's *Guide to the Bodhisattva Way of Life*

The Wolf Shall Dwell with the Lamb

The wolf shall dwell with the lamb,
and the leopard shall lie down with the kid,
and the calf and the lion and the fatling together,
and a little child shall lead them.
The cow and the bear shall feed;
their young shall lie down together;
and the lion shall eat straw like the ox.
The suckling child shall play over the hole of the asp,
and the weaned child shall put his hand on the adder's den.
They shall not hurt or destroy in all my holy mountain;
for the earth shall be full of the knowledge of the Lord
as the waters cover the sea.

— Isaiah 11:6–9

SENDING FORTH

The work is not ended. It has just begun. Let us now go out to share, in whatever way we feel is best, our message of care for the Earth.

A Jewish Blessing

With mercy You give light to the world and to its inhabitants.
In your goodness You renew creation day after day.
How manifold are Your works, O Lord.
With wisdom You fashioned them all.
The earth abounds with Your creations, Eternal God,
our shield and protection,
Lord of our strength,
rock of our defense.
You whose mercy is without bounds,
forgive us and continue to love us.
In magnificence, reflecting Your splendor,
You created the sun and sent forth its rays.
The lights of the heaven radiate Your glory.
The hosts of heaven exalt You and recount Your holiness.
As we marvel at the stars so radiant with light,
as we wonder at all life that You have created,
we glorify You, Lord our God.

— Rabbi Hertzberg

A Christian Blessing

Most high, all-powerful, all good Lord!
All praise is yours, all glory, all honor
And all blessing.
To you alone, Most High, do they belong.
No mortal lips are worthy
To pronounce your name.
All praise be yours, my Lord,
through all that you have made:
Brother Sun, Sister Moon and Stars,
Brothers Wind and Air,
Sister Water, Brother Fire,
All praise be yours, my Lord,
through Sister Earth, our Mother,
Who feeds us in her sovereignty and produces
Various fruits with colored flowers and herbs.

All praise be yours, my Lord, through all those who respect your creatures, our brothers and sisters.

May this celebration remind us of the wisdom, beauty, and love that you, my Lord, have poured onto all your works.

May this celebration summon us to a frugal use of earthly goods and arouse within us a desire for spiritual joy.

May this celebration lead men and women into the paths of justice, peace, and reconciliation.

May you be blessed, my Lord, in all your angels and saints.

— Father Lanfranco Serrini

At the end bells are rung to announce to the world what has taken place, that the alliance between religion and environmentalism has again been affirmed.

10

A LITURGY FOR THE EARTH

CALL TO PRAYER

O Great Spirit,
Whose breath gives life to the world
and whose voice is heard in the soft breeze,
we need your strength and wisdom.
May we walk in Beauty.
May our eyes ever behold the red and purple sunset.
Make us wise so that we may understand what you have taught us.
Help us learn the lessons you have hidden in every leaf and rock.
Make us always ready to come to you with clean hands and straight eyes
so when life fades, as the fading sunset,
our spirits may come to you without shame.

— From a Native American prayer

Leader: The Earth is the Lord's and the fullness thereof,

All: The world and all those who dwell in it.

THE SORROW OF THE EARTH

Leader: The litany we will now use draws upon the symbolism of
the American Indian people. Because the Earth is the source
of blessings — food, clothing, shelter, the seasons, healing
medicines, beauty — and is the nurturer of life, the Earth is

Adapted from a service prepared for Church Women United, by a group of Native American women.

personified in myth and poetry and called "mother." God, the creator and source of all life, is called Great Spirit. Mother Earth speaks:

Voice: Listen, my children. The Spirit who moved over the dry land is not pleased. I am thirsty. Are you listening?

All: We are listening, Mother Earth. Speak.

Voice: The Spirit who filled the waters is not pleased. I choke with debris and pollution. Are you listening?

The Spirit who brought beauty to the Earth is not pleased. The Earth grows ugly with misuse. Are you listening?

The Spirit who brought forth all the creatures is being destroyed. Are you listening?

The Spirit who gave humans life and a path to walk together is not pleased. You are losing you humanity and your footsteps stray from the path. Are you listening?

Leader: Let us pray. O God, you created the Earth in goodness and in beauty. Forgive all that we have done to harm the Earth. O God, you have filled the Earth with food for our sustenance. Forgive us for not sharing the gifts of the Earth. You have created us, O God, of one blood throughout the Earth. Forgive us for not living as sisters and brothers should.

— Sister Mary Rosila Shiosee, S.B.S.

THE HEALING OF EARTH'S WOUNDS

Leader: Great Spirit, whose dry lands thirst, help us to find the way to refresh your lands.

All: We pray for your power to refresh your lands.

Leader: Great Spirit, whose waters are choked with debris and pollution, help us to find the way to cleanse your waters.

All: We pray for your knowledge to find the way to cleanse the waters.

Leader: Great Spirit, whose beautiful Earth grows ugly with misuse, help us to find the way to restore the beauty of your handiwork.

All: We pray for your strength to restore the beauty of your handiwork.

Leader: Great Spirit, whose creatures are being destroyed, help us to
             find the way to replenish them.

All: We pray for your power to replenish the Earth.

Leader: Great Spirit, whose gifts to us are being lost in selfishness and
             corruption, help us to find the way to restore our humanity.

All: We pray for your wisdom to find the way to restore our
             humanity.

                          . . . Silent Reflection . . .

All: Great Spirit, give us hearts to understand;
             never to take from creation's beauty more than we give;
             never to destroy wantonly for the furtherance of greed;
             never to deny to give our hands
             for the building of Earth's beauty;
             never to take from her what we cannot use.
             Give us hearts to understand
             that to destroy Earth's music is to create confusion;
             that to wreck her appearance is to blind us to beauty;
             that to callously pollute her fragrance
             is to make a house of stench;
             that as we care for her she will care for us. Amen.

DISMISSAL

All: Now Talking God,
             With your feet I walk,
             I walk with your limbs,
             I carry forth your body,
             For me your mind thinks,
             Your voice speaks for me.
             Beauty is before me
             And beauty is behind me.
             Above and below me hovers the beautiful,
             I am surrounded by it,
             I am immersed in it.
             In my youth I am aware of it,
             And in old age
             I shall walk quietly
             The beautiful trail.

11

RETELLING THE RAINBOW
A Meal for Earth and Water, Air and Fire

Each table is set with a clear pitcher of clear water in the center; a plate bearing brown rice, red beans, yellow cornbread, black bread, and whole-wheat matzah (unleavened bread); a bowl bearing different fruit of varied colors; seven candles, each a different color of the rainbow; and a prism or crystal that refracts light into its spectrum.

Begin with a song about the Earth and caring for it. Other songs may also be used during the retelling, when participants wish.

Then — turn out all lights. In the darkness, a speaker:

In the beginning, darkness covered the face of the deep.
Then the rushing-breath of life hovered over the waters.
[*Pause...*] Let us breathe together.
[*Pause...*] Let us catch our breaths from the need to *make*, to *do*.
[*Pause...*] Let us be conscious of the Breath of Life.
[*Pause...*] We breathe out what the trees breathe in.
[*Pause...*] We breathe in what the trees breathe out.
[*Pause...*] Together we breathe each other into life.
[*Pause...*] Blessed is the One within the many.
Blessed are the Many who make one.

Another speaker:

And the darkness gave birth to light.

Light the seven candles at each table. All say, together:

We are the generation that stands between the fires:
behind us the flame and smoke
that rose from Auschwitz and from Hiroshima;
before us the nightmare of a Flood of Fire,
the flame and smoke that could consume all Earth.
It is our task to make from fire not an all-consuming blaze
but the light in which we see each other fully.
All of us different,
all of us bearing One Spark.
We light these fires to see more clearly
that the Earth and all who live as part of it
are not for burning.
We light these fires to see more clearly
the rainbow in our many-colored faces.

Blessed is the One within the many.
Blessed are the Many who make one.

The youngest present points to the food, water, etc. in the center of the table and says:

Why is this night different from all other nights?
On all other nights we eat one kind of bread;
tonight we eat from grains and breads and fruits of many colors.
On all other nights we drink water, wine, or milk;
tonight we drink only water.
On all other nights we see in light of whiteness;
tonight we see in lights of many colors.
On all other nights we breathe however we like;
tonight we began by pausing to breathe together.

An elder responds:

Our foods come from the Earth; we come from many lands.
The water unites us.
The lights are fire; what burns in our hearts is varied.
The air unites us.

The youngest present, picking up the prism and making the colors flash:

Tell me the story of the rainbow!

Readers (one reader reads each of the stanzas below, and then another takes up the story for the next stanza):*

Now the Earth had gone to ruin before God,
the Earth was filled with wrongdoing.
God saw the Earth, and here: it had gone to ruin,
for all flesh had ruined its way upon the Earth.

God said to Noah ["Restful-one"]:
An end of all flesh has come before me,
for the Earth is filled with wrongdoing through them;
here, I am about to bring ruin upon them, along with the Earth.
Make yourself an Ark of *gofer* wood,
with reeds make the Ark,
and cover it within and without with a covering-of-pitch.

As for me,
here, I am about to bring on the Flood, water upon the Earth,
to bring ruin upon all flesh that has breath of life in it,
from under the heavens,
all that is on Earth will perish.
But I will establish my covenant with you:
you are to come into the Ark,
you and your sons and your wife and your sons' wives with you,
and from all living-things, from all flesh,
you are to bring two from all into the Ark, to remain alive with you.
They are to be a male and a female each,
from fowl after their kind, from herd-animals after their kind,
from all crawling things of the soil after their kind,
two from all are to come to you, to remain alive.
As for you,
take for yourself from all edible-things that are eaten and gather it to you,
it shall be for you and for them, for eating.

Noah ["Restful-one"] did it,
according to all that God commanded him, so he did.
And Noah ["Restful-one"] came,
his sons and his wife and his sons' wives with him,
into the Ark before the waters of the Flood.

---

*The passages from Genesis are based on the translation by Everett Fox, *In the Beginning* (New York: Schocken, 1983), with some changes: "Human" is always in this retranslation connected with "earthy," because in Hebrew "adamah" means "earth" and "adam" means "human being." "Earth/earthling" or "human/humus" would catch something of this relationship in English. The Hebrew name "Noah" comes from the root that means "rest" or "restful." "Yahh / Breath of Life" is used to represent "YHWH," the Name of Divinity in Its most intimate and loving aspect. The nearest we can come to pronouncing this Name, as well as to expressing its deep meaning, is by breathing only — without a specific name or word. "God" is used as the translation for "Elohim," but it might be more accurate to translate it as "Divinity" or "Creative-Power."

They and all wildlife after their kind,
all herd-animals after their kind,
all crawling things that crawl upon the Earth after their kind,
all fowl after their kind, all chirping-things, all winged-things;
they came to Noah ["Restful-one"] into the Ark,
two and two each from all flesh in which is breath of life.
And those that came, male and female from all flesh they came,
as God had commanded him.
Yahh / the Breath of Life enclosed him.

●

A reader:

Within us and without,
between us and beyond,
is the breath of life:
We breathe each other into being.

Those present let themselves become conscious of their breath, perhaps with their eyes closed. They breathe out, letting their lungs empty, and pause; they breathe in, letting their lungs fill, and pause.

A reader:

What is the story of the breath of life?

Those present comment on any aspect of the story up to now: "Restful-one," the ruining of the Earth, the role of Noah's family, the Ark, the breath of life.

●

A reader begins again:

In the second New-Moon,
on the seventeenth day of the New-Moon, on that day:
then burst all the well-springs of the great Ocean
and the sluices of the heavens opened up.
The Flood was forty days upon the Earth.
The waters increased and lifted the Ark,
so that it was raised above the Earth;
the waters swelled and increased exceedingly upon the Earth,
so that the Ark floated upon the face of the waters.
When the waters had swelled exceedingly, yes, exceedingly over the Earth,
all high mountains that were under all the heavens were covered.

Then perished all flesh that crawls about upon the Earth —
fowl, herd-animals, wildlife,
and all swarming things that swarm upon the Earth,
and all earthy-human beings;
all that had rush or breath of life in their nostrils,

all that were on firm ground, died.
God blotted out all existing-things that were on the face of the Earth,
from human to animal, to crawling thing and to fowl of the heavens,
they were blotted out from the Earth.
Noah ["Restful-one"] alone remained,
and those who were with him in the Ark.
The waters swelled upon the Earth for a hundred and fifty days.
But God paid mind to Noah ["Restful-one"] and all living-things,
all the animals that were with him in the Ark,
and God brought a breath-of-wind across the Earth,
so that the waters abated.
The well-springs of Ocean
and the sluices of the heavens were dammed up,
and the torrent from the heavens was held back.

•

A reader, pointing to the bowls of water on the table:

These waters, why do we gather them?

Someone else:

We gather the rains and the Ocean
for these waters are waters of drowning,
and these waters are waters of birthing,
and these waters are waters of life:
Let us drink!

One person at the table ceremoniously pours water from the pitcher into the glass of the next person, and then passes the pitcher to that person, who pours for the next one and then passes the pitcher on. When the circle is complete, everyone lifts a glass with both hands, and all say together:

Blessed is the One within the many.
Blessed are the Many who make one.

All drink from their own glasses.

Those present comment on the story of water: how the water sounded and felt and tasted when they drank, what they remember of too little water and too much water, when their waters broke in birthing.

•

The reading begins again:

The waters returned from upon the Earth,
continually advancing and returning,
and the waters diminished at the end of a hundred and fifty days.
And the Ark came to rest in the seventh New-Moon,
on the seventeenth day of the New-Moon,

upon the mountains of Ararat.
Now the waters continued to advance and diminish
until the tenth New-Moon.
On the tenth, on the first day of the New-Moon,
the tops of the mountains could be seen.

At the end of forty days it was:
Noah ["Restful-one"] opened the window of the Ark that he had made,
and sent out a raven;
it went off, going off and returning,
until the waters were dried up from upon the Earth.
Then he sent out a dove from him,
to see whether the waters had subsided from the face of the soil.
But the dove found no resting-place for the sole of her foot,
so she returned to him into the Ark,
for there was water upon the face of all the Earth.
He sent forth his hand and took her, and brought her to him into the Ark.
Then he waited yet another seven days
and sent out the dove yet again from the Ark.
The dove came back to him at eventime,
and here — a freshly plucked olive leaf in her beak!
So Noah ["Restful-one"] knew
that the waters had subsided from upon the Earth.
Then he waited yet another seven days and sent out the dove,
but she returned to him again no more.

And so it was in the six hundred and first year,
in the beginning-month, on the first day of the New-Moon,
that the waters left firm ground upon the Earth.
Noah ["Restful-one"] removed the covering of the Ark and saw:
here, the face of the Earth was firm.

Now in the second New-Moon,
on the twenty-seventh day of the New-Moon,
the Earth was completely dry.
God spoke to Noah ["Restful-one"], saying:
Go out of the Ark, you and your wife,
your sons and your sons' wives with you.
All living-things that are with you, all flesh —
fowl, animals, and all crawling things that crawl upon the Earth,
have them go out with you,
that they may swarm on Earth,
that they may bear fruit and become many upon the Earth.
So Noah ["Restful-one"] went out,
his sons, his wife, and his sons' wives with him,

all living-things — all crawling things, and all fowl,
all that crawl about upon the Earth,
according to their clans they went out of the Ark.
And Yahh / the Breath of Life said, heart-felt:
I will never doom the Earth again on earthy-humankind's account,
since what the earthy human heart forms is evil from its youth;
I will never again strike down all living-things, as I have done;
never again, all the days of the Earth, shall

> sowing and harvest,
> cold and heat,
> summer and winter,
> day and night
> ever cease!

God said to Noah ["Restful-one"] and to his sons with him:
As for me — here, I am about to establish my covenant with you
and with your seed after you,
and with all living beings that are with you:
fowl, herd-animals, and all the wildlife of the Earth with you;
all those going out of the Ark, of all the living-things of the Earth.
I will establish my covenant with you:

> All flesh shall never be cut off again by waters of the Flood,
> never again shall there be Flood, to bring the Earth to ruin!

And God said:
This is the sign of the covenant which I set
between me and you and all living beings that are with you,
for ageless generations:
My bow I set in the clouds,
so that it may serve as a sign of the covenant between me and the Earth.
It shall be:
when I becloud the Earth with clouds
and in the clouds the bow is seen,
I will call to mind my covenant
that is between me and you and all living beings — all flesh:

> never again shall the waters become a Flood,
> to bring all flesh to ruin!

When the bow is in the clouds,
I will look at it,
to call to mind the age-old covenant
between God and all living beings —
all flesh that is upon the Earth.

God said to Noah ["Restful-one"]:
This is the sign of the covenant that I have established
between me and all flesh that is upon the Earth.

•

Someone reaches for the prism in the middle of the table. All say together:

Blessed is the One within the many.
Blessed are the Many who make one.

The prism is passed from hand to hand around the table, and each participant makes it flash the colors of the rainbow.

*A reader:**

For love is strong as death,
Harsh as the grave.
Its tongues are flames, a fierce
And holy blaze.

Endless seas and floods,
Torrents and rivers
Never put out love's
Infinite fires.

All together:

For love is the fire
That blazes in the Rainbow.

Those present comment or question on fire, light, the meaning of the rainbow.

A reader:

In our oldest memories
is carved the danger
that the human race might work such ruin
as to sweep away all life upon this planet.
In our own generation
we tremble on the verge of Flood.

Another reader:

In our own generation
we tremble on the verge of Flood.

The air is full of poison.
The rain, the seas, are full of poison.
The Earth hides arsenals of poisonous fire,
seeds of light surcharged with fatal darkness.
The ice is melting,
the seas are rising,
the air is dark with smoke and rising heat.

---

*The passages from the Song of Songs here and on p. 106 are from Marcia Falk, *The Song of Songs: A New Translation and Interpretation* (HarperSanFrancisco, 1990). Copyright © 1990 by Marcia Lee Falk.

Another reader:

Who speaks for the redwood and the rock, the lion and the beetle?
Who are our Noahs?
Who can teach us to be "Restful-ones"?
Where is our Ark?
Who can renew the Rainbow?

What must we do to reaffirm
the covenant between the Breath of Life
and all who live and breathe upon this planet?

Who speaks for the redwood and the rock, the lion and the beetle?
Who are our Noahs?
Who can teach us to be "Restful-ones"?
Where is our Ark?
Who can renew the Rainbow?

Pause for reply, comment, questions, discussion from all who are at the table on any issue that has touched them — and especially on the nature and meaning of Flood, Ark, and Rainbow in our own lives and the life of the Earth today. Some may wish to speak in the persona not of human being but of a bird, a fish, a beetle, a mountain, a tree that is at risk of Flood upon the planet.

In particular, invite those present to make commitments — covenants — of what action they will take to protect the Earth.

When the discussion seems ready to end, another reader:

We are earthlings, who spring from the Earth.
We are earthlings, who live on the Earth and from it.
We are earthlings, and the Earth feeds us.
We are earthlings, and we feed the Earth.

Someone passes the platter of breads, grains, and beans.

A reader:

May the many colors of our fruitful Earth
nourish the many colors of our fruitful earthlings.

All together:

Blessed is the One within the many.
Blessed are the Many who make one.

All eat from the bread, by putting a slice or chunk of bread directly in the mouth of someone else, who does the same in return.

There may again at this point be time for discussion of these different foods, their different bio-regional origins, their different colors, tastes, textures, how they are grown, how they have affected life on the planet.

Dinner may begin at this point, and the discussion can continue during it.

At the end of dinner, someone passes the bowl of fruit, and each person takes one or a few different ones.

A reader:
Come with me,
my love,
come away

For the long wet months are past,
the rains have fed the Earth
and left it bright with blossoms

Birds wing in the low sky,
dove and songbird singing
in the open air above

Earth nourishing tree and vine,
green fig and tender grape,
green and tender fragrance

Come with me,
my love,
come away

. . . finding our doorways piled with fruits,
The best of the new-picked and the long-stored,
My love, I will give you all I have saved for you.

All say:

Blessed is the One within the many.
Blessed are the Many who make one.

All eat from the fruit.

Following the meal, sing "Rise and Shine" or other appropriate songs.

12

PRAYER SERVICE

A CALL TO PRAYER

We who have lost our sense and our senses —
Our touch, our smell, our vision of who we are;
we who frantically force and press all things,
without rest for body or spirit,
hurting our Earth and injuring ourselves: We call a halt.

We want to rest.
We need to rest and allow the Earth to rest.
We need to reflect and to rediscover the mystery that lives in us,
that is the ground of every unique expression of life,
the source of the fascination that calls all things to communion.

We declare an Earth Holy Day, a space of quiet:
for simple being and letting be;
for recovering the great forgotten truths.

A PRAYER OF AWARENESS

Today we know of the energy that moves all things:
the oneness of existence,
the diversity and uniqueness of every moment of creation,
every shape and form,

This prayer service was written by Rev. Daniel Martin, religious consultant to the United Nations Conference on Environment and Development.

the attraction, the allurement,
the fascination that all things have for one another.

Humbled by our knowledge,
chastened by surprising revelations,
with awe and reverence we come before the mystery of life.

A PRAYER OF SORROW

Reader 1:   We have forgotten who we are;
we have alienated ourselves from the unfolding of the cosmos;
we have become estranged from the movements of the Earth;
we have turned our backs on the cycles of life.

Reader 2:   We have sought only our own security;
we have exploited simply for our own ends;
we have distorted our knowledge;
we have abused our power.

Reader 3:   Now the land is barren,
and the waters are poisoned,
and the air is polluted.

Reader 4:   Now the forests are dying,
and the creatures are disappearing,
and the humans are despairing.

Reader 5:   We ask forgiveness;
we ask for the gift of remembering;
we ask for the strength to change.

. . . Silence . . .

A PRAYER OF HEALING

Reader 1:   We join with the Earth and with each other
to bring new life to the land,
to restore the waters,
to refresh the air

Reader 2:   To renew the forests,
to care for the plants,
to protect the creatures

Reader 3:   To celebrate the seas,
to rejoice in the sunlight,
to sing the song of the stars

Reader 4:   To recall our destiny,
            to renew our spirits,
            to reinvigorate our bodies

Reader 5:   To create the human community,
            to promote justice and peace,
            to remember our children.

Leader: We join together as many and diverse expressions
            of one loving mystery:
            for the healing of the Earth and the renewal of all life.

...Meditation...

A PRAYER OF GRATITUDE

Reader 1:   We rejoice in all life.
            We live in all things.
            All things live in us.

Reader 2:   We live by the sun.
            We move by the stars.

Reader 3:   We eat from the Earth.
            We drink from the rain.
            We breathe from the air

Reader 4:   We share with the creatures.
            We have strength through their gifts.

Reader 5:   We depend on the forests.
            We have knowledge through their secrets.

Reader 6:   We have the privilege of seeing and understanding.
            We have the responsibility of caring.
            We have the joy of celebrating.

Leader: We are graceful.
            We are grateful.
            We rejoice in all life.

A GUIDED MEDITATION FOR THE FULLNESS OF CREATION

WHO ARE WE?

WE ARE THE EARTH. [*Be conscious of the Earth beneath your feet and the feel of your body where it contacts...*]

Earth is stardust-come-to-life, a magic cauldron where the heart of the universe is being formed. In me, the Earth and its creatures find their voices. Through my eyes the stars look back on themselves in wonder. I am the Earth. This is my body. *Listen and remember.*

WE ARE THE AIR. [*Be conscious of breathing...*]

Air is the breath of the Earth, the movement of life, the quick, violent storm, and the slow, caressing breeze. In my breathing, life is received and given back. My breath unites me to all things, to the creatures that make the oxygen, and to the people who share the same breath: yesterday a victim of AIDS; today a soldier in the Middle East; tomorrow, a poor woman in the Third World. I am air. This is my breath. *Listen and remember.*

WE ARE FIRE. [*Be conscious of inner activity, of thoughts and emotions...*]

By Rev. Daniel Martin. From *The Episcopal Church in Communion with Creation: Policy and Action Plan for the Environment and Sustainable Development*, Report of the Presiding Bishop's Consultation on the Environment and Sustainable Development in preparation for the General Convention of 1991, September 1990. Used with permission of the author and the Program for the Environment, Cathedral of St. John the Divine, New York.

Fire is the energy of the universe, the source of power and new life. In my thoughts burn the fires of the original eruption of life; in my emotions, lightning flashes; in my love, new life is conceived. I participate in power. I share in the energy of the universe, to keep warm, to fuel my body, to create my relationships. I am fire. This is my power. *Listen and remember.*

WE ARE WATER. [*Be conscious of saliva, sweat, tears . . .*]

Water is the womb of the Earth from which all life is born. The oceans flow through the Earth, bringing abundance; the oceans flow through me, carrying food, recycling waste, expressing emotions. I am water. This is my life. *Listen and remember.*

BUT WE HAVE FORGOTTEN WHO WE ARE.

In our mindlessness, we are corrupting the Earth, poisoning the air, disrupting the fire, polluting the water. We are making life impossible for our fellow creatures and for ourselves. We are destroying the heart of the universe.

> Come Holy Spirit of Earth, air, fire, and water.
> Enkindle in us the fire of your love.
> Send your spirit over the waters and we shall be created.
> And we shall renew the face of the Earth.

14

PRAYERS AND
SHORT READINGS

A Prayer for Conservation

Giver of life and all good gifts:
Grant us also wisdom to use only what we need;
Courage to trust your bounty;
Imagination to preserve our resources;
Determination to deny frivolous excess;
And inspiration to sustain through temptation.

— Patricia Winters

Blessed Treasures

Help us to harness
the wind,
the water,
the sun,
and all the ready
and renewable
sources of power.

Teach us to conserve,
preserve,
use wisely
the blessed treasures
of our wealth-stored earth.

Help us to share
your bounty,
not to waste it,
or pervert it
into peril
for our children
or our neighbors
in other nations.

You who are life
and energy
and blessing,
teach us to revere
and respect
your tender world.

— Thomas John Carlisle

A Few Feet in Diameter

If the Earth were only a few feet in diameter, floating a few feet above a field somewhere, people would come from everywhere to marvel at it. People would walk around it, marvelling at its big pools of water, its little pools and the water flowing between the pools. People would marvel at the bumps on it, and the holes in it, and they would marvel at the very thin layer of gas surrounding it and the water suspended in the gas. The people would marvel at all the creatures walking around the surface of the ball, and at the creatures in the water. The people would declare it as sacred because it was the only one, and they would protect it so that it would not be hurt. The ball would be the greatest wonder known, and people would come to pray to it, to be healed, to gain knowledge, to know beauty and to wonder how it could be. People would love it, and defend it with their lives; their own roundness, could be nothing without it. If the earth were only a few feet in diameter.

— From Coyote Point Museum for Environmental Education
and Friends of the Earth, New Zealand

FROM THE NATIVE AMERICAN TRADITION

Teach Your Children

Teach your children what we have taught our children,
that the Earth is our mother.
Whatever befalls the Earth, befalls the children of the Earth.
If we spit upon the ground, we spit upon ourselves.
This we know.
The Earth does not belong to us; we belong to the Earth.
One thing we know, which the white man may one day discover,
our God is the same God.
You may think now that you own God as you wish to own our land,
but you cannot.
God is the God of all people,
and God's compassion is equal for all.
This Earth is precious to God,
and to harm the Earth is to heap contempt on its Creator.
So love it as we have loved it.
Care for it as we have cared for it.
And with all your mind, with all your heart,
preserve it for your children . . . as God loves us all.

— Attributed to Chief Sealth of the Suquamish, approximately 1855

How Can You Buy or Sell the Sky?

How can you buy or sell the sky, the warmth of the land?
The idea is strange to us.
Every part of this Earth is sacred to my people.
Every shining pine needle,
every sandy shore,
every mist in the dark woods,
every clearing and humming insect
is holy in the memory and experience of my people.
The sap which courses through the trees
carries the memories of the red man.
The shining water that moves in the streams and rivers
is not just water but the blood of our ancestors.

If we sell you land,
you must remember that it is sacred,
and you must teach your children that it is sacred,
and that each ghostly reflection in the clear water of the lake
tells of events and memories in the life of my people.
The water's murmur is the voice of my father's father.
The rivers are our brothers, they quench our thirst.
The rivers carry our canoes, and feed our children.
If we sell you our land,
you must remember, and teach your children,
that the rivers are our brothers, and yours,
and you must henceforth give the rivers the kindness
you would give your brother.

And what is man without the beasts?
If the beasts were gone,
men would die from a great loneliness of spirit.
For whatever happens to the beasts, soon happens to man.
All things are connected. This we know.
The Earth does not belong to man; man belongs to the Earth.
This we know.
All things are connected like the blood which unites one family.
All things are connected.

> — Attributed to Chief Sealth of the Suquamish, 1854, to mark the
> transferral of ancestral Indian lands to the federal government

Chinook Blessing Litany

We call upon the Earth, our planet home,
with its beautiful depths and soaring heights,
its vitality and abundance of life,
and together we ask that it:
     Teach us, and show us the way.

We call upon the mountains, the Cascades and the Olympics,
the high green valleys and meadows filled with wild flowers,
the snows that never melt, the summits of intense silence,
and we ask that they:
     Teach us, and show us the way.

We call upon the land which grows our food,
the nurturing soil, the fertile fields,
the abundant gardens and orchards,
and we ask that they:
     Teach us, and show us the way.

We call upon the forests,
the great trees reaching strongly to the sky
with Earth in their roots and the heavens in their branches,
the fir and the pine and the cedar,
and we ask them to:
      Teach us, and show us the way.

We call upon the creatures of the fields and forests and the seas,
our brothers and sisters the wolves and deer,
the eagle and dove,
the great whales and the dolphin,
the beautiful Orca and salmon
who share our Northwest home,
and we ask them to:
      Teach us, and show us the way.

We call upon all those who have lived on this Earth,
our ancestors and our friends,
who dreamed the best for future generations,
and upon whose lives our lives are built,
and with thanksgiving we call upon them to:
      Teach us, and show us the way.

And lastly, we call upon all that we hold most sacred,
the presence and power of the Great Spirit of love and truth
which flows through all the universe . . .
to be with us to:
      Teach us, and show us the way.

—Chinook Learning Center, Whidbey Island, Wash.

Give Us Hearts to Understand

Great Spirit, give us hearts to understand:
never to take
from creation's beauty more than we give;
never to destroy wantonly for the furtherance of greed;
never to deny to give our hands for the building of Earth's beauty;
never to take from her what we cannot use.
Give us hearts to understand
that to destroy Earth's music is to create confusion;
that to wreck her appearance is to blind us to beauty;
that to callously pollute her fragrance is to make a house of stench;
that as we care for her she will care for us.
Amen.

Grandfather, Look at Our Brokenness

Grandfather,
Look at our brokenness.

We know that in all creation
Only the human family
Has strayed from the Sacred Way.

We know that we are the ones
Who are divided
And we are the ones
Who must come back together
To walk in the Sacred Way.

Grandfather,
Sacred One,
Teach us love, compassion, and honor
That we may heal the Earth
And heal each other.

— Ojibway Prayer

FROM THE MUSLIM TRADITION

Everything Is Sacred

Under Islam, everything is created by Allah (God) and therefore everything is sacred, useful, and has its place in the general scheme of things and in the interest of humankind.

The protection of God's creation is therefore the duty of the Muslims and God will reward all who protect creation.

God has created the skies, the earth, the sun and the moon, the rivers and the mountains. God has created the animals and vegetables, the birds, the fish and all that exists between the earth and sky!

The totality of the environment is God's creation and humankind's responsibility to protect.

The Holy Quran declares, "We have created everything from water." Hence the importance of water resources for human life. The survival of human life also depends upon agriculture and animal husbandry. Hence the Muslim obligation to be kind to animals and grateful for the availability of the rivers and the rain. Indeed, there are special prayers for rain in which Muslims express appreciation for God's bounty and beg God to continue it by providing the faithful with rain.

The relationship of Muslims to God is a direct and simple one. Muslims call upon their Creator for everything: When we are sick, we pray for God to provide us with health. If we are poor and hungry, we beg God for food and support, and so on. Hence, the permanent link between humankind and the environment through God and prayers to the Creator.

Islam is a religion that started in the deserts of Arabia with a universal message. Its concern for the environment is a universal concern, cutting across national, religious, and geographical barriers. Its major commandments are directed, not to the Muslims, but to the human race. Hence its call upon "people" (not the Arabs nor the Muslims) to conserve the natural resources as God's gift to humankind.

There are many verses from the Holy Quran and Hadith (statements by the Prophet), urging people to be kind to the land, to the rivers, to the air, and not to abuse the fertile valleys. Kindness to "those who cannot speak" (animals) is urged by the Prophet again and again.

In his letter of recommendation, the First Muslim Khalifa, Abu-Baker, ordered his troops, "Do not cut down a tree, do not abuse a river, do not harm animals, and be always kind and humane to God's creation, even to your enemies."

Muslim commitment to the sanctity of life is most pronounced during the Haj to Mecca, where the pilgrims are not permitted even to kill an insect.

Under Islam, the individual is responsible for the "good" and for the "bad." *En Ahsantum, Ahsantum le-Anfosekum wa en Asaatum fa-lahaa* (If you do good things, you do that for yourselves, and if you do wrong things, that is for you, too!) Hence, the responsibility for the protection of the environment is an individual responsibility in the first place and a "collective" obligation of the society secondarily.

Following is a Muslim prayer for rain, called "Prayer for 'Istesquaa' " . . . begging God for rain.

> O God! The Creator of everything!
> You have said that water is the source of all life!
>> When we have needs, You are the Giver.
>> When we are sick, You give us health.
>> When we have no food, You provide us with your bounty.
>
> And so God, presently, we have no rain. We need water.
> Our water resources are dry; we need you to help us with rain —
> rain for our fields, our orchards, and our animals.
> We need water for ablution and general cleanliness
> to prepare for worshipping You, O Lord.
>
> Our confidence, O Lord, is in you
> and your unlimited mercy and compassion.
> Please, Merciful God, provide us with rain.

> — Dr. Mohammed Mehdi

When the Sun Shall Be Folded Up

When the sun shall be folded up,
and when the stars shall fall,
and when the mountains shall be set in motion,
and when the she-camels shall be abandoned,
and when the wild beasts shall be gathered together,
and when the seas should boil,
and when the souls shall be paired with their bodies,
and when the female child that had been buried alive shall be asked
for what crime she was put to death,
and when the leaves of the Book shall be unrolled,
and when the Heaven shall be stripped away,
and when Hell shall be made to blaze,

and when Paradise shall be brought near,
every soul shall know that it hath produced. . . .
Whither then are ye going?
Verily, this is no other than a warning to all creatures.

— *The Koran* LXXXI

FROM THE JEWISH TRADITION

The Covenant

And it shall come to pass,
when I bring clouds over the earth,

and the bow is seen in the cloud,
that I will remember My covenant,

which is between Me and you
and every living creature of all flesh;

and the waters shall no more
become a flood to destroy all flesh.

— Genesis 9:8–17

Forging a New Land Ethic from the Bible

The Jewish tradition grew out of the relationship between a people and their land, or to shift the lens, between a land and its people. Take yourself back three thousand years. Our lives revolved around the seasons and the cycle of the sun: Planting and harvesting, praying for rain in the winter and dew in the summer.

Like ecology, Judaism teaches that every act has a consequence. We do not live in a vacuum. Rather, the universe is one interconnected, interdependent whole, and the future depends on our being responsible for our acts in the present.

There are hundreds of laws in Judaism that specifically concern themselves with the environment. The most famous of the laws is called *Bal Tashchit* — do not destroy. This law, based on a passage in Deuteronomy, commands even during war not to cut down trees, "for the human is the tree of the field."

The tree is the archetypical life symbol in Judaism. With its roots reaching deep into the soil for nourishment and its branches reaching high up into the sky, the tree is a symbol that life is an interdependent progress between an organism and everything it touches. At the same time, the passage also notes that humans are like trees and are part of a global field, affected by and affecting the atmosphere, the water and vegetation. In the situation of war, which we might perceive as life or death for our people, the Torah is saying there is something more important to consider than cutting down trees for human need: The life of the whole planetary organism.

What we ecologists have been saying for the last twenty years and what the Torah has been saying indirectly for the last three thousand, we are now experiencing in our own backyards. You can't throw something away because there is no such place as away. We live in a web of cycles, and one way or another things come back to us through poisoned air and overflowing landfills.

I often think of the words of Isaiah: Without vision, the people perish, I contend we desperately need a vision. It is the vision of a more perfect world that will propel us into creating that world.

— Ellen Bernstein

Among All Growing Things

Grant me the ability to be alone;
may it be my custom to go outdoors each day
among the trees and grasses,
among all growing things,
and there may I be alone,
and enter into prayer
to talk with the one
that I belong to.

— Rabbi Nachman of Bratzlav

The First Human Being

Why was the first human being called Adam? Rabbi Yehuda says: By virtue of the earth (Adamah) from which Adam was taken.

— Midrash Hagadol Bereshit

Finish Your Planting

If you are in the midst of planting and word reaches you that the Messiah has arrived, do not interrupt your work; first finish your planting, and only then go out to welcome the Messiah.

— Rabbi Yochanan Ben Zakai

Just to Be Is a Blessing

Just to be is a blessing.
Just to live is holy.

— Rabbi Abraham Heschel

The Earth Dries Up and Withers

The earth dries up and withers
the world languishes and withers,
the heavens languish together
with the earth.
The earth lies polluted
under its inhabitants;
for they have transgressed laws,
violated the statutes,
broken the everlasting covenant.

— Isaiah 24:4–5

FROM THE CHRISTIAN TRADITION

The Earth Is at the Same Time Mother

The earth is at the same time mother,
She is mother of all that is natural,
         mother of all that is human.

She is mother of all,
for contained in her
are the seeds of all.

The earth of humankind
contains all moistness,
         all verdancy,
         all germinating power.

It is in so many ways fruitful.
All creation comes from it.
Yet it forms
not only the basic raw material
for humankind,
but also the substance
of the incarnation
of God's son.

— Hildegard of Bingen

Be a Gardener

Be a gardener.
Dig a ditch,
toil and sweat,
and turn the earth upside down
and seek the deepness
and water the plants in time.
Continue this labor
and make sweet floods to run
and noble and abundant fruits
to spring.

Take this food and drink
and carry it to God
as your true worship.

—Julian of Norwich

Hymn of the Universe

I live at the heart of a single, unique Element, the Center of the Universe, and present in each part of it: personal Love and cosmic Power.

To attain to Him and become merged into his life I have before me the entire universe with its noble struggles, its impassioned quests, its myriad of souls to be healed and made perfect. I can and I must throw myself into the thick of human endeavor, and with no stopping for breath. For the more fully I play my part and the more I bring my efforts to bear on the whole surface of reality, the more also will I attain to Christ and cling close to him. God who is eternal Being-in-itself, is, one might say, ever in process of formation for us.

And God is also the heart of everything; so much so that the vast setting of the universe might be engulfed or wither away or be taken from me by death without my joy being diminished. Were creation's dust, which is vitalized by a halo of energy and glory, to be swept away, the substantial Reality wherein the rays originate would be drawn back onto their Source and there I should still hold them all in a close embrace.

—Pierre Teilhard de Chardin

I Am the One

I am the one
whose praise echoes on high.
I adorn all the earth.

I am the breeze
that nurtures all things green.
I encourage blossoms
to flourish with ripening fruits.

I am led by the spirit
to feed the purest streams.

I am the rain
coming from the dew
that causes the grasses to laugh
with the joy of life....
I am the yearning for good.

—Hildegard of Bingen

A Prayer of Awareness

God is the foundation
for everything.

This God undertakes,
God gives,

Such that nothing
that is necessary
for life
is lacking.

Now humankind needs a body
that at all times honors
and praises God.

This body is supported in every way
through the earth.

Thus the earth glorifies
the power of God.

— Hildegard of Bingen

Peace with All of Creation

In our day, there is a growing awareness that world peace is threatened not only by the arms race, regional conflicts, and continued injustices among peoples and nations, but also by a lack of due respect for nature, by the plundering of natural resources, and by a progressive decline in the quality of life. The sense of precariousness and insecurity that such a situation engenders is a seedbed for collective selfishness, disregard for others, and dishonesty.

Faced with the widespread destruction of the environment, people everywhere are coming to understand that we cannot continue to use the goods of the earth as we have in the past....

Certain elements of today's ecological crisis reveal its moral character. First among these is the indiscriminate application of advances in science and technology. Many recent discoveries have brought undeniable benefits to humanity. Indeed, they demonstrate the nobility of the human vocation to participate responsibly in God's creative action in the world.

Unfortunately, it is now clear that the application of these discoveries in the fields of industry and agriculture have produced harmful long-term effects. This has led to the painful realization that we cannot interfere in one area of the ecosystem without paying due attention both to the consequences of such interference in other areas and to the well-being of future generations....

In 1979, I proclaimed St. Francis of Assisi as the heavenly patron of those who promote ecology. He offers Christians an example of genuine and deep respect for the integrity of creation. As a friend of the poor who was loved by God's creatures, St. Francis invited all creation — animals, plants, natural forces, even Brother Sun and Sister Moon — to give honor and praise to the Lord. The poor man of Assisi gives us striking witness that when we are at peace with God we are better able to devote ourselves to building up that peace with all creation, which is inseparable with peace among all peoples.

— Pope John Paul II, message for the World Day of Peace,
January, 1, 1990

Prayer of Confession

Gracious God,
who made the covenant promise with our ancestors,
we gather here today a rebellious people.
We want to act out your intentions for us,
but we keep getting mixed up
by all the glitter of the world around us.
You tell us to honor creation,
and we use other people and animals and plant life
only to meet our wants.
You offer daily bread to every living creature,
and we steal that bread from our brothers and sisters
in the name of our greed.
You promise us new life,
and we shrink back from it in fear.
Heal us, God, lest we destroy ourselves.
We need your presence among us. Amen.

— From UN *Environmental Sabbath*

Canticle of Brother Sun, Sister Moon

Most high omnipotent, good Lord,
Thine are all praise, glory, honor, and all benedictions,
To Thee alone, Most High, do they belong
And no man is worthy to name Thee.

Praise be to Thee, My Lord, with all Thy creatures,
Especially Brother Sun,
Who is our day and lightens us therewith.
Beautiful is he and radiant with great splendor;
Of Thee, Most High, he bears expression.

Praise be to Thee, my Lord,
for Sister Moon, and for the stars
in the heavens which Thou has formed
bright, precious, and fair.

Praise be to Thee, my Lord,
for Brother Wind,
And for the air and the cloud of fair
and all weather
Through which Thou givest
sustenance to Thy creatures.

Praise be, my Lord, for Sister Water.
Who is most useful, humble, precious, and chaste.

Praise be, my Lord, for Brother Fire,
by whom Thou lightest up the night:
He is beautiful, merry, robust and strong.

Praise be, my Lord, for our sister,
Mother Earth,
who sustains and governs us
and brings forth diverse fruits and
many-hued flowers and grass.

— St. Francis

Three-Way Covenant

The Book of Genesis reveals that when the Flood ended and the Earth was cleansed, God made a Covenant with Noah — of which the sign was the rainbow.

Today, most of us remember of that Covenant only that it made peace between God and humankind. But there was more to it than that; for the Covenant was not between God and ourselves alone. It was a *three-party* Covenant — and *Nature* was the third party:

> Behold, I establish my Covenant
> with you and your descendants,
> *and with every living creature that is with you . . .*
> *every beast of the Earth . . .*
>
> When I bring clouds over the Earth
> and the bow is seen in the clouds . . .
> I will look on it and remember the everlasting Covenant
> between God and *every* living creature on the Earth.

What does it mean, that the Covenant included Nature? It means Nature was promised Peace, too — God's Peace, which *should* have included Peace with humanity as well.

The Book of Genesis that has come down to us today does not spell out the way in which we humans are to keep that Peace with nature. But God has never ceased to speak in our hearts, and if we listen, God will teach us all we need to know.

Listen, then: not with your outward ears alone, but with every atom of your inward being. Listen as the Hebrews did, to the wind they called *Ruakh*, which is the Spirit of the LORD and the Breath by which we live. Listen to the fountain from which your life arises. Listen in the stillness of your heart.

Thus I have heard:

> I the LORD am the God that made you; and as I made you, so have I made all living things, and a fit place for each living thing, and a world for all living things to share in interdependence.

> And my reasons for making all these are one with my reasons for making you:

>> that each living thing may rejoice in its own being,
>> and in the company of all beings,
>> and in me, the sum and essence and fulfillment of being,
>> whose name is I AM THAT AM;
>> and that I may rejoice in each living thing,
>> and in the company of all living things,
>> which I have blessed and hallowed with my love
>> and to which I have lent a measure of that Light
>> by which you know that I am near.

> All living things I have included in that Covenant I made with your ancestors long ago; and by that Covenant I gave them rights and a place, which you must not deny them, lest you displease your God.

> And so that my Creation may be cherished, and my Covenant honored, and my love made manifest, and you regain sight of who you truly are, thus I command:

> You shall not act in ignorance of the ecological consequences of your acts.

> You shall not seek such ignorance, nor hide in such ignorance, hoping to say afterward, "Forgive me, for I knew not what I did"; for there will be no forgiveness of willful ignorance or self-deception, either in this world or in any other.

You shall not keep others in ignorance of the ecological consequences of their acts; for their ecological wrongdoing will be reckoned against you as if it were your own.

You shall not act in any way which makes the world less able to sustain life:

> not by destroying the soil,
> nor by destroying the living sea,
> nor by laying waste to wild places,
> nor by releasing poisons,
> nor by causing great changes in the climate.

You shall not act in any way that injures the buffers I have set about this world to protect its life:

> the ozone layer of the atmosphere,
> the carbon dioxide sink of the sea,
> the chemical balance of the waters,
> the interface between water and sky,
> the vegetative cover of hillside and plain,
> the multitude of species in a region,
> the balance of species, each with each,
> the adaptability of species, as contained in their genes.

You shall not exterminate any living species,

> nor destroy the niche wherein it dwells,
> nor remove its existence from that niche,
> nor render it incapable of dwelling that niche.

You shall not encroach on a species' niche, nor destroy its natural defenses, nor reduce its numbers, to the point where its survival is endangered.

And as I forbid these acts to you, so I forbid you to place others in a position where they must commit such acts; for their ecological wrongdoing will be reckoned against you as if it were your own.

I am the creator of this world; treasure it as your Father's treasure.

Honor the life of all living things, and the order of Nature, and the wildness of wilderness,

> and the richness of the created world,
> and the beauty of lands undefiled by your works;
> and seek the holiness I have placed in these things,
> and the measure of Light I have lent them;

and preserve these things well;
for all these are my gifts to you from the dawn of time,
and their like will not be offered you again.

And in the fulfillment of these commandments, be not half-hearted, and do not err on the side of your greed and your convenience; but act with all your ability to love,

> and all your ability to discern,
> and all your ability to understand,
> and all your ability to foresee;
> for I know your capacities,
> and I will know how well you make use of them.

And if you will listen carefully to my voice, and accept my guidance in all these matters, and obey and honor and fulfill these commandments, not in the letter only but in the fullness of truth,

> then I will bless your life,
> and the lives of all about you,
> and all that you hold dear.

I will bless you in your arising and your midday and your evening, and bless your sleep, and sweeten all your dreaming;

I will bless your settlements and your cultivations, and the wild places you will never see;

I will add to your riches, and multiply your happiness;

From generation to generation you will witness the unfolding of the future I myself have planned for the world from the beginning of time, and your hearts will overflow with the joy of it.

But if you will not attend to me, and instead live contrary to my way, your own acts and choices will become the means of your undoing.

Then it will seem to you that all the world has hardened and turned against you, though it is only that you have cast yourself out of the Covenant of the world;

Famine and thirst, drought and flood and storm, blight and plague, divisions and strife, and slow painful death will walk among you;

Your house will be cast down, your fields laid waste, and all memory of your existence blotted out.

And on the day these punishments arrive, do not think to bargain with the LORD for mercy; for these punishments will come out of the law I established at the dawn of time, the very laws through which I made you a place in my creation, and these laws are a part of the Covenant, which I have pledged never to set aside.

Therefore be holy, as I who love and dwell within you am holy.

I am the LORD.

> — Marshall Massey, The Peaceable Kingdom Project,
>   Society of Friends

FROM THE BUDDHIST TRADITION

The Rain Cloud

It is like a great cloud rising above the world,
covering all things everywhere —
a gracious cloud full of moisture;
lightning-flames flash and dazzle,
voice of thunder vibrates afar,
bringing joy and ease to all.
The sun's rays are veiled,
and the earth is cooled;
the cloud lowers and spreads
as if it might be caught and gathered;
its rain everywhere equally descends on all sides,
streaming and pouring unstinted, permeating the land.
On mountains, by rivers, in valleys,
in hidden recesses, there grow the plants, trees, and herbs;
trees, both great and small,
the shoots of the ripening grain,
grape vine and sugar cane.
Fertilized are these by the rain and abundantly enriched;
the dry ground is soaked;
herbs and trees flourish together.
From the one water which issued from that cloud,
plants, trees, thickets, forests,
according to need receive moisture.
All the various trees, lofty, medium, low,
each according to its size,
grow and develop roots, stalks, branches, leaves,
blossoms and fruits in their brilliant colors;
wherever the one rain reaches,
all become fresh and glossy.
According as their bodies, forms, and natures are great and small,
so the enriching rain,
though it is one and the same,
yet makes each of them flourish.
In like manner also the Buddha appears here in the world
like unto a great cloud universally covering all things;

and having appeared in the world,
for the sake of the living,
he discriminates and proclaims the truth in regard to all laws.
The Great Holy World-Honored One among the gods and humans,
and among all living beings proclaims abroad this word:
"I am the Tathagata,
the Most Honored among humans;
I appear in the world like this great cloud,
to pour enrichment on all parched living beings,
to free them from their misery to attain the joy of peace,
joy of the present world and joy of Nirvana ...
Everywhere impartially, without distinction of persons ...
ever to all beings I preach the Law equally; ...
equally I rain the Law — rain untiringly."

                        — From the Lotus Sutra

FROM THE HINDU TRADITION

The Waters, Who Are Goddesses

They who have the ocean as their eldest flow out of the sea,
purifying themselves, never resting.
Indra, the bull with the thunderbolt, opened a way for them;
let the waters, who are goddesses, help me here and now.

The waters of the sky or those that flow,
those that are dug out or those that arise by themselves,
those pure and clear waters that seek the ocean as their goal —
let the waters, who are goddesses, help me here and now.

Those in whose midst King Varuna moves,
looking down upon the truth and falsehood of people,
those pure and clear waters that drip honey —
let the waters, who are goddesses, help me here and now.

Those among whom King Varuna, and Soma,
and all the gods drink in ecstasy the exhilarating nourishment,
those into whom Agni of-all-men entered —
let the waters, who are goddesses, help me here and now.

— From the Rig Veda

Let Us Be United

Let us be united;
let us speak in harmony;
let our minds apprehend alike.
Common be our prayer;
common be the end of our assembly;
common be our resolution;
common be our deliberations.
Alike be our feelings;
unified be our hearts;
common be our intentions;
perfect be our unity.

— From the Rig Veda

Prayer for Peace

Supreme Lord,
let there be peace in the sky and in the atmosphere,
peace in the plant world and in the forests;
let the cosmic powers be peaceful;
let Brahma be peaceful;
let there be undiluted and fulfilling peace everywhere.

— Atharvaveda

FROM THE CHINESE TRADITION

If Your Are Thinking

If you are thinking a year ahead, sow seed.
If you are thinking ten years ahead, plant a tree.
If you are thinking a hundred years ahead, educate the people.

— Kuan-Tsu, third century B.C.E.

Nothing Is Weaker Than Water

In the world there is nothing more submissive and weak than water.
Yet for attacking that which is hard and strong nothing can surpass it.
This is because there is nothing that can take its place.

That the weak overcomes the strong,
and the submissive overcomes the hard,
everyone in the world knows;
yet no one can put this knowledge into practice.

Therefore the sage says,
One who takes on himself the humiliation of the state
is called a ruler worthy of offering sacrifices to the gods of earth and millet;
one who takes on himself the calamity of the state
is called a king worthy of dominion over the entire empire.

Straightforward words
seem paradoxical.

— Lao Tzu, *Tao Te Ching*, LXXVIII

FROM THE BAHA'I TRADITION

Spiritual Foundations for an Ecologically Sustainable Society

The transformative power of the Baha'i vision rests in its conception of the unity of material and spiritual evolution. Within this vision, the ecological interdependence of life on earth can be understood as the physical representation of a unifying spiritual reality. Humanity is part of this communion of life, and the material and spiritual development of civilization is part of a collective planetary process. The long historical process of becoming conscious beings through separation from Nature is culminating in the scientific understanding of life's profound interrelatedness.

It is in this unifying context that humanity's current destructive relationship to Nature must be placed. The prevailing social order is based on separation from and control over Nature, because it represents an adolescent phase in the progressive development of civilization. Having passed from the dependence of childhood through the impetuous, autonomy-seeking stage of adolescence, humanity is now at the point of transition to conscious maturity. . . .

Our work will truly become worship when our spiritual and technical capacities are consecrated to serving the whole of life. With this consciousness, human beings will become co-creators with Nature of the Kingdom of God. . . .

Restoring a vision of wholeness in our relationship to Nature and of spiritual purpose in the whole evolution of life gives a basis for creating a life-affirming culture. It gives a reason to trust life and human capacities for faith and creativity. It gives a positive context for the design of life-sustaining rather than life-depleting production systems. It encourages the release of spiritual potential in individuals so that they can become agents of transformation in the world while furthering the evolution of their own souls. All of these are aspects of the integration of inner spiritual and outer material realities, and all are involved in developing an ecologically sustainable society.

— Robert A. White, "Spiritual Foundations
for an Ecologically Sustainable Society"

PART FOUR

Who Will Save the Earth?

A two-day interfaith convocation in Assisi in 1986 celebrated the twenty-fifth anniversary of the World Wildlife Fund. In the spirit of medieval Europe, banners waving, bells sounding, representatives of the world's five major religions gathered in concern for the environment. Photo: WWF/H.J. Burkard/Bilderberg.

15

THE ASSISI DECLARATIONS

❀

THE EVENT AT ASSISI*

In autumn 1986, a unique alliance was forged between conservation and five of the world's great religions. The venue was Assisi, in central Italy. The event marked the twenty-fifth anniversary of the World Wildlife Fund, the world's largest private nature conservation organization, and involved many of the hundreds of groups that WWF had worked with over the past quarter century. With a pilgrimage, conference, cultural festival, retreat, and interfaith ceremony in the Basilica of St. Francis, the events of Assisi formed the launching pad for a permanent alliance between conservation and religion.

For religions, ecological problems pose major challenges in relating theology and belief to the damage to nature and human suffering caused by environmental degradation. All too often, religious teaching has been used or abused to justify the destruction of nature and natural resources.

In the declarations issued at Assisi, leading religious figures mapped out the way to re-examine and reverse this process. At the same time, starting with the conference and retreat held in Assisi, religious philosophers are helping to inject some powerful moral perspectives into conservation's ill-defined ethical foundations.

---

*Reprinted from the *Bulletin* of the WWF Network on Conservation and Religion, no. 1, Winter 1986/87.

THE BUDDHIST DECLARATION ON NATURE
Venerable Lungrig Namgyal Rinpoche
Abbot, Gyuto Tantric University

Homage to Him whose vision and speech
Made Him unexcelled as a sage and teacher;
The being who saw the interdependence of Nature,
And taught it to the world!

In the words of the Buddha Himself: "Because the cause was there, the consequences followed; because the cause is there, the effects will follow." These few words present the interrelationship between cause (karma) and its effects. It goes a step further and shows that happiness and suffering do not simply come about by chance or irrelevant causes. There is a natural relationship between a cause and its resulting consequences in the physical world. In the life of the sentient beings too, including animals, there is a similar relationship of positive causes bringing about happiness and negative actions causing negative consequences. Therefore, a human undertaking motivated by a healthy and positive attitude constitutes one of the most important causes of happiness, while undertakings generated through ignorance and negative attitude bring about suffering and misery. And this positive human attitude is, in the final analysis, rooted in genuine and unselfish compassion and loving kindness that seeks to bring about light and happiness for all sentient beings. Hence Buddhism is a religion of love, understanding, and compassion, and committed towards the ideal of nonviolence. As such, it also attaches great importance to wildlife and the protection of the environment on which every being in this world depends for survival.

The simple underlying reason why beings other than humans need to be taken into account is that, like human beings, they too are sensitive to happiness and suffering; they too, just like the human species, primarily seek happiness and shun suffering. The fact that they may be incapable of communicating their feelings is no more an indication of apathy or insensibility to suffering or happiness than in the case of a person whose faculty of speech is impaired. Yet it would appear from past history that the opposite view has been predominant.

Hence many have held up usefulness to human beings as the sole criterion for the evaluation of an animal's life. Upon closer examination one discovers that this mode of evaluation of another's life and fight for existence has also been largely responsible for human indifference as well as cruelty to animals, not to speak of violence in today's world. On sober reflection, one can find that there is a striking similarity between exterminating the life of a wild animal for fun and terminating the life of an innocent fellow human being at the whim of a more capable and powerful person. We should therefore be wary of justifying the right of any species to survive solely on the basis of its usefulness to human beings.

Many additional factors contribute to and reinforce this insight in Buddhism. A philosophical system which propagates the theory of rebirth and life after death, it maintains that in the continuous birth and rebirth of sentient beings (not only on this planet but in the universe as a whole) each being is related to us ourselves, just as our own parents are related to us in this life. And just as our own parents have been indispensable to our upbringing in our present lifespan, in another particular span of our life another particular sentient being has given us the spark of life. The fact that we are totally unaware of such a relationship does not undermine this observation any more than the idea that a particular person is not someone's parent simply because they do not realize the connection.

We are told that history is a record of human society in the past. From existing sources there is evidence to suggest that for all their limitations, people in the past were aware of this need for harmony between human beings and nature. They loved the environment. They revered it as the source of life and well-being in the world. In my faraway country, I still remember what my parents said: they told us that various spirits and forces are dormant in the rivers, mountains, lakes, and trees. Any harm done to them, they said, would result in drought, epidemics, and sickness in human beings, and the loss of fertility of the Earth.

We regard our survival as an undeniable right. As co-inhabitants of this planet, other species too have this right for survival. And since human beings as well as other nonhuman sentient beings depend upon the environment as the ultimate source of life and well-being, let us share the conviction that the conservation of the environment, the restoration of the imbalance caused by our negligence in the past, be implemented with courage and determination.

These teachings lead us to the following words by His Holiness the Dalai Lama:

> As we all know, disregard for the natural inheritance of human beings has brought about the danger that now threatens the peace of the world as well as the chance of endangered species to live.
>
> Such destruction of the environment, and the life depending upon it, is a result of ignorance, greed, and disregard for the richness of all living things. This disregard is gaining great influence. If peace does not become a reality in the world and if the destruction of the environment continues as it does today, there is no doubt that future generations will inherit a dead world.
>
> Our ancestors have left us a world rich in its natural resources and capable of fulfilling our needs. This is a fact. It was believed in the

past that the natural resources of the Earth were unlimited, no matter how much they were exploited. But we know today that without understanding and care these resources are not inexhaustible. It is not difficult to understand and bear the exploitation done in the past out of ignorance, but now that we are aware of the dangerous factors, it is very important that we examine our responsibilities and our commitment to values and think of the kind of world we are to bequeath to future generations.

It is clear that this generation is at an important crossroad. On the one hand the international community is able now to communicate each other's views, on the other hand the common fact is that confrontation far outweighs constructive dialogue for peace.

Various crises face the international community. The mass starvation of human beings and the extinction of species may not have overshadowed the great achievements in science and technology, but they have assumed equal proportions. Side by side with the exploration of outer space, there is the continuing pollution of lakes, rivers, and vast parts of the oceans, out of human ignorance and misunderstanding. There is a great danger that future generations will not know the natural habitat of animals; they may not know the forests and the animals that we of this generation know to be in danger of extinction.

We are the generation with the awareness of a great danger. We are the ones with the responsibility and the ability to take steps of concrete action, before it is to late.

THE HINDU DECLARATION ON NATURE
His Excellency Dr. Karan Singh
President, Hindu Virat Samaj

In the ancient spiritual traditions, man was looked upon as part of nature, linked by indissoluble spiritual and psychological bonds with the elements around him. This very much marked the Hindu tradition, probably the oldest living religious tradition in the world. The Vedas, those collections of hymns composed by great spiritual seers and thinkers which are the repository of Hindu wisdom, reflect the vibrance of an encompassing worldview which looks upon all objects in the universe, living or nonliving, as being pervaded by the same spiritual power.

Hinduism believes in the all-encompassing sovereignty of the divine, manifesting itself in a graded scale of evolution. The human race, though at the top of the evolutionary pyramid at present, is not seen as something apart from the Earth and its multitudinous life forms. The Atharva Veda has the magnificent Hymn to the Earth, which is redolent with ecological and environmental values. The following verses are taken from this extraordinary hymn:

> Earth, in which lie the sea, the river, and other waters,
> in which food and cornfields have come to be,
> in which lives all that breathes and that moves,
> may she confer on us the finest of her yield.

> Earth, in which the waters, common to all,
> moving on all sides, flow unfailingly, day and night,
> may she pour us milk in many streams,
> and endow us with luster.

> May those born of thee, O Earth,
> be for our welfare, free from sickness and waste.
> Wakeful through a long life, we shall become
> bearers of tribute to thee.

> Earth, my mother, set me securely with bliss
> in full accord with heaven.
> O wise one,
> uphold me in grace and splendor.

Not only in the Vedas, but in late scriptures such as the Upanishads, the Puranas, and subsequent texts, the Hindu viewpoint on nature has been clearly enunciated. It is permeated by a reverence for life and an awareness that the great forces of nature — the earth, the sky, the air, the water and fire — as well as various orders of life including plants and trees, forests and animals, are all bound to each other within the great rhythms of nature. The divine is not exterior to creation, but expresses itself through natural phenomena. Thus in the Mundaka Upanishads the divine is described as follows:

> Fire is his head, his eyes are the moon and the sun;
> the regions of space are his ears, his voice the revealed Veda;
> the wind is his breath, his heart is the entire universe;
> the Earth is his footstool, truly he is the inner soul of all.

In addition, according to the Vaishnava tradition, the evolution of life on this planet is symbolized by a series of divine incarnations beginning with fish, moving through amphibious forms and mammals, and then on into human incarnations. This view clearly holds that man did not spring fully formed to dominate the lesser life forms, but rather evolved out of these forms itself, and is therefore integrally linked to the whole of creation.

This leads necessarily to a reverence for animal life. The Yajurveda lays down that "no person should kill animals helpful to all. Rather, by serving them, one should attain happiness" (Yajurveda 13:47). This view was later developed by the great Jain Tirthankara, Lord Mahavira, who regenerated the ancient Jain faith that lives down to the present day. For the Jains, Ahimsa, or nonviolence, is the greatest good and on no account should life be taken. This philosophy was emphasized more recently by Mahatma Gandhi, who always spoke of the importance of Ahimsa and looked upon the cow as a symbol of the benign element in animal life. All this strengthens the attitude of reverence for all life, including animals and insects.

Apart from this, the natural environment also received the close attention of the ancient Hindu scriptures. Forests and groves were considered sacred, and flowering trees received special reverence. Just as various animals were associated with gods and goddesses, different trees and plants were also associated in the Hindu pantheon. The Mahabharata says that "even if there is only one tree full of flowers and fruits in a village, that place becomes worthy of worship and respect." Various trees, fruits, and plants have special significance in Hindu rituals.

The Hindu tradition of reverence for nature and all forms of life, vegetable or animal, represents a powerful tradition which needs to be renurtured and reapplied in our contemporary context. India, the population of which is over 80 percent Hindu, has in recent years taken a special interest in conservation.

What is needed today is to remind ourselves that nature cannot be destroyed without mankind ultimately being destroyed itself. With nuclear weapons representing the ultimate pollutant, threatening to convert this beautiful planet of ours into a scorched cinder unable to support even the most primitive life forms, mankind is finally forced to face its dilemma. Centuries of rapacious exploitation of the environment have finally caught up with us, and a radically changed attitude towards nature is now not a question of spiritual merit or condescension, but of sheer survival.

This Earth, so touchingly looked upon in the Hindu view as the Universal Mother, has nurtured mankind up from the slime of the primeval ocean for billions of years. Let us declare our determination to halt the present slide towards destruction, to rediscover the ancient tradition of reverence for all life and, even at this late hour, to reverse the suicidal course upon which we have embarked. Let us recall the ancient Hindu dictum: "The Earth is our mother, and we are all her children."

THE JEWISH DECLARATION ON NATURE
Rabbi Arthur Hertzberg
Vice-President, World Jewish Congress

"Whoever is merciful to all creatures is a descendant of our ancestor Abraham" (Bezoh 32b). In the sacred writings of Judaism, Jews are described over and over again as "merciful people, the children of merciful people"

(Yebamor 79a, Shabbat 133b). The Talmud even tells us (Shabbat 151b) that heaven rewards the person who has concern and compassion for the rest of creation, but this assurance of reward is not the major moral thrust of Jewish teaching. Our tradition emphasized that Jews are commanded to do what is moral, "not for the sake of receiving a reward" (Abot 1:3). The good is necessary even when it does not redound to our immediate, personal benefit.

When God created the world, so the Bible tells us, He made order out of primal chaos. The sun, the moon, and the stars, plants, animals, and ultimately man, were each created with a rightful and necessary place in the universe. They were not to encroach on each other. "Even the divine teaching, the Torah, which was revealed from on high, was given in a set measure" (Vayikra Rabbah 15:2) and even these holy words may not extend beyond their assigned limit. "And the Lord took man and put him in the Garden of Eden, to tend it and guard it" (Genesis 2:15). Soon Adam, man, the one creature who is most godlike, gave names to all of creation, as God looked on and approved. "And the name that Adam gave to each living being has remained its name" (Genesis 2:19) forever. In the Kabbalistic teaching, as Adam named all of God's creatures, he helped define their essence. Adam swore to live in harmony with those whom he had named. Thus, at the very beginning of time, man accepted responsibility before God of all creation.

Judaism, of course, knows the doctrine of the world beyond death, but its central concern is with life in the world. The tzaddik, the righteous Jew, is not a pillar saint who has withdrawn from the world. He is someone whose conduct in the very midst of life helps to establish that which seems impossible — one can live in this world of righteousness without encroaching on the rights of other people, or of any of God's creatures.

The festivals of the Jewish religion do call upon us to stand before God, in awe at His majesty, trembling before His judgments, but that is not the dominant mood of the Jewish faith. The festivals celebrate, in joy, the cycle of the seasons of nature. The rabbis even insisted that: "He who has denied himself any one of the rightful joys of this world is a sinner" (Baba Kama 91b). The highest form of obedience to God's commandments is to do them not in mere acceptance but in the nature of union with Him. In such a joyous encounter between man and God, the very rightness of the world is affirmed.

The encounter of God and man in nature is thus conceived in Judaism as a seamless web with man as the leader and custodian of the natural world. Even in the many centuries when Jews were most involved in their own immediate dangers and destiny, this universalist concern has never withered. In this century, Jews have experienced the greatest tragedy of their history when one-third of their people were murdered by unnatural men and, therefore, we are today particularly sensitive to the need for a world in which each of God's creations is what He intended it to be. Now, when the whole world is in peril, when the environment is in danger of being poisoned and various species, both plant and animal, are becoming extinct, it is our Jewish responsibility to put the defense of the whole of nature at the very center of our concern.

And yet it must be said, in all truth, that this question of man's responsibility to the rest of creation cannot be defined by simply expressing our respect for all of nature. There is a tension at the center of the biblical tradition, embedded in the very story of creation itself, over the question of power and stewardship. The world was created because God willed it, but why did He will it? Judaism has maintained, in all of its versions, that this world is the arena that God created for man, half beast and half angel, to prove that he could be a moral being. The Bible did not fail to demand even of God Himself that He be bound, as much as man, by the law of mortality. Thus, Abraham stood before God, after He announced that He was about to destroy the wicked city of Sodom, and Abraham demanded of God Himself that He produce moral justification for this act: "Shall not the judge of all the earth do justice?" (Genesis 18:25). Comparably, man was given dominion over nature, but he was commanded to behave towards the rest of creation with justice and compassion. Man lives, always, in tension between his power and the limits set by his conscience.

Man's carnivorous nature is not taken for granted, or praised, in the fundamental teachings of Judaism. The rabbis of the Talmud told that men were vegetarian in earliest times, between creation and the generation of Noah. In the twelfth century Maimonides, the greatest of all rabbinic scholars, explained that animal sacrifices had been instituted in ancient Judaism as a concession to the prevalent ancient practice of making such offerings to the pagan gods (Mareh Nebuhim 111:32). The implication is clear that Judaism was engaged in weaning men from such practices.

Judaism as a religion offers the option of eating animal flesh, and most Jews do, but in our own century there has been a movement towards vegetarianism among very pious Jews. A whole galaxy of central rabbinic and spiritual teachers, including several past and present Chief Rabbis of the Holy Land, have been affirming vegetarianism as the ultimate meaning of Jewish moral teaching. They have been proclaiming the autonomy of all living creatures as the value which our religious tradition must now teach to all of its believers. Let this affirmation resound this day and in days to come. Let it be heard by all our brethren, wherever they may be, as the commandment which we must strive to realize. This cannot be achieved in one generation, and it will not happen through pressure from within or without. Jews will move increasingly to vegetarianism out of their own deepening knowledge of what their tradition commands, as they understand it in this age.

Our ancestor Abraham inherited his passion for nature from Adam. The later rabbis never forgot it. Some twenty centuries ago they told the story of two men who were out on the water in a rowboat. Suddenly, one of them started to saw under his feet. He maintained that it was his right to do whatever he wished with the place which belonged to him. The other answered him that they were in the rowboat together; the hole that he was making would sink both of them (Vayikra Rabbah 4:6).

We have a responsibility to life, to defend it everywhere, not only against our own sins but also against those of others. We are all passengers together in this same fragile and glorious world. Let us safeguard our rowboat — and let us row together.

THE MUSLIM DECLARATION ON NATURE
His Excellency Dr. Abdullah Omar Nasseef
Secretary General, Muslim World League

The essence of Islamic teaching is that the entire universe is God's creation. Allah makes the waters flow upon the Earth, upholds the heavens, makes the rain fall, and keeps the boundaries between day and night. The whole of the rich and wonderful universe belongs to God, its maker. It is God who created the plants and the animals in their pairs and gave them the means to multiply. Then God created mankind — a very special creation because mankind alone was created with reason and the power to think and even the means to turn against his Creator. Mankind has the potential to acquire a status higher than that of the angels or sink lower that the lowliest of the beasts.

The word "Islam" has the dual meaning of submission and peace. Mankind is special, a very particular creation of Allah. But still we are God's creation and we can only properly understand ourselves when we recognize that our proper condition is one of submission to the God who made us. And only when we submit to the Will of God can we find peace: peace within us as individuals, peace between man and man, and peace between man and nature. When we submit to the Will of God, we become aware of the sublime fact that all our powers, potentials, skills and knowledge are granted to us by God. We are his servants and when we are conscious of that, when we realize that all our achievements derive from the Mercy of God, when we return proper thanks and respect and worship God for our nature and creation, then we become free. Our freedom is that of being sensible, aware, responsible trustees of God's gifts and bounty.

For the Muslim, mankind's role on Earth is that of *khalifa*, viceregent or trustee of God. We are God's stewards and agents on Earth. We are not masters of this Earth; it does not belong to us to do what we wish. It belongs to God and He has entrusted us with its safekeeping. Our function as viceregents, *khalifa* of God, is only to oversee the trust. The *khalifa* is answerable for his/her actions, for the way in which he/she uses or abuses the trust of God.

Islam teaches us that we have been created by God and that we will return to God for Judgment; that we are accountable for our deeds as well as our omissions. The *khalifa* will render an account of how he treated the trust of God on the Day of Reckoning. The notion that describes the accountability of the *khalifa* is *akhrah*. Islam is the guidance of how to live today so that we can face the *akhrah*; it is the Message which informs us of what will be involved in the reckoning.

The central concept of Islam is *tawheed,* or the Unity of God. Allah is Unity, and His Unity is also reflected in the unity of mankind and the unity of man and nature. His trustees are responsible for maintaining the unity of His creation, the integrity of the Earth, its flora and fauna, its wildlife and natural environment. Unity cannot be had by discord, by setting one need against another or letting one end predominate over another; it is maintained by balance and harmony in the whole of creation around us.

So unity, trusteeship, and accountability, that is *tawheed, khalifa,* and *akhrah,* the three central concepts of Islam, are also the pillars of the environmental ethics of Islam. They constitute the basic values taught by the Qur'an. It is these values which led Muhammad, the Prophet of Islam, to say: "Whoever plants a tree and diligently looks after it until it matures and bears fruit is rewarded," and "If a Muslim plants a tree or sows a field and men and beasts and birds eat from it, all of it is charity on his part," and again, "The world is green and beautiful and God has appointed you his stewards over it." Environmental consciousness is born when such values are adopted and become an intrinsic part of our mental and physical makeup.

And these are not remote, otherworldly, notions; they concern us here and now. If you were to ask me what the notion of the Hereafter has to do with here and now, my answer might surprise you. I would say nuclear power and biotechnology. Both of these are very present here-and-now issues. Both have benefits and costs. Both have implications for the health and well-being of mankind and nature. If I sincerely intend to be God's *khalifa,* His steward on Earth, then I must have an opinion about them, must prepare myself to make choices about them, because I will be accountable for what mankind has wrought with these devices in the Hereafter.

Islam is a very practical worldview. It seeks, in all its principles and injunctions, to give pragmatic shapes to its concepts and values. Indeed, the notions of *tawheed* and *khalifa* have been translated into practical injunctions in the *Shariah.* Such *Shariah* institutions as *haram* zones, inviolate areas within which development is prohibited to protect natural resources, and *hima,* reserves established solely for the conservation of wildlife and forests, form the core of the environmental legislation of Islam. The classical Muslim jurist, Izz ad-Din ibn Abd as-Salam, used these aspects of the *Shariah* when he formulated the bill of the legal rights of animals in the thirteenth century. Similarly, numerous other jurists and scholars developed legislations to safeguard water resources, prevent overgrazing, conserve forests, limit the growth of cities, protect cultural property, and so on. Islam's environmental ethics than are not limited to metaphysical notions; it provides a practical guide as well.

Muslims need to return to this nexus of values, this way of understanding themselves and their environment. The notions of unity, trusteeship, and accountability should not be reduced to matters of personal piety; they must guide all aspects of their life and work. *Shariah* should not be relegated just to issues of crime and punishment; it must also become the vanguard for environmental legislation. We often say that Islam is a complete way of life, by which it is meant that our ethical system provides the bearings for all our actions. Yet our actions often undermine the very values we cherish. Often while working as scientists or technologists, economists or politicians, we act contrary to the environmental dictates of Islam. We must imbibe these values into our very being. We must judge our actions by them. They furnish us with a worldview which enables us to ask environmentally appropriate questions, draw up the right balance sheet of possibilities, properly weigh the environmental costs and benefits of what we want, what we can do within the ethical boundaries established by God, without violating the rights of His other creations. If we use the same values, the same understanding in our work as scientist or technologist, economist or politician as we do to know ourselves as Muslims — those who submit themselves to the Will of God — then, I believe, we will create a true Islamic alternative, a caring and practical way of being, doing and knowing, to the environmentally destructive thought and action which dominates the world today.

THE CHRISTIAN DECLARATION ON NATURE
Father Lanfranco Serrini
Minister General, O.F.M. Conv.

"Praise the Lord! . . . Praise him, sun and moon, praise him, all you shining stars! For he commanded and they were created. . . . Praise the Lord from the earth, you sea monsters and all deeps, fire and hail, snow and frost, stormy wind fulfilling his commands!" (Psalm 148)

To praise the Lord for his creation is to confess that God the Father made all things visible and invisible; it is to thank him for the many gifts he bestows on all his children.

God created everything that exists, freely, by his word, and out of nothing. He alone is totally other, transcendent, and immutable, whereas all creatures are contingent, mutable, and wholly dependent on him for their existence. No creature can claim to be part of his nature or a "spark" of his Being; but, by reason of its created origin, each according to its species and all together in the harmonious unity of the universe manifest God's infinite truth and beauty, love and goodness, wisdom and majesty, glory and power.

God declared everything to be good, indeed, very good. He created nothing unnecessarily and has omitted nothing that is necessary. Thus, even in the mutual opposition of the various elements of the universe, there exists a divinely willed harmony because creatures have received their mode of existence by the will of their Creator, whose purpose is that through their interdependence they should bring to perfection the beauty of the universe. It is the very nature of things considered in itself, without regard to man's convenience or inconvenience, that gives the glory to the Creator.

But it is especially through man and woman, made in the image and likeness of God and entrusted with a unique dominion over all visible creatures, that the Lord's goodness and providence are to be manifested. This is how the Psalmist sings of man's nobility: "When I look at the heavens, the work of your fingers, the moon and the stars which you have established; what is man that you are mindful of him, and the son of man that you care for him? Yet, you have made him little less than God, and you crown him with glory and honor. You have given him dominion over the works of your hands" (Psalm 8:3–6).

The Fathers of the Church understood well the marvel of man's dual citizenship and the responsibilities it placed upon him. In the words of St. Gregory of Nazianzen, "God set man upon earth as a kind of second world, a microcosm; another kind of angel, a worshipper of blended nature. . . . He was king of all upon earth, but subject to heaven; earthly and heavenly; transient, yet immortal; belonging both to the visible and to the intelligible order; midway between greatness and lowliness." Most certainly, then, because of the responsibilities which flow from his dual citizenship, man's dominion cannot be understood as license to abuse, spoil, squander, or destroy what God has made to manifest his glory. That dominion cannot be anything other than a stewardship in symbiosis with all creatures. On the one hand, man's position verges on a viceregal partnership with God; on the other, his self-mastery in symbiosis with creation must manifest the Lord's exclusive and absolute dominion over everything, over man and over his stewardship. At the risk of destroying himself, man may not reduce to chaos or disorder, or, worse still, destroy God's bountiful treasures.

Every human act of irresponsibility towards creatures is an abomination. According to its gravity, it is an offense against that divine wisdom which sustains and gives purpose to the interdependent harmony of the universe.

Christians believe that the first man's refusal to live according to divine wisdom introduced disharmony into his relationship with God and creatures, and this rebellion has perpetuated itself in history in various forms of social and personal injustice, domination, and exploitation, making it impossible for men and women to live in concord with one another and with the rest of creation.

But the heart of Christian faith resides in its proclamation of God's merciful fidelity to himself and to the works of his hands. Christians believe that God the Father has not abandoned men and women to their sinful ways but has sent the Savior to bring redemption and healing to everyone and to all things. Indeed, they firmly confess that Jesus of Nazareth is the Son of God made man, that he is the fulfillment of his Father's covenant with Abraham for the salvation of all peoples and with Noah on behalf of all creation. They maintain that, risen from the dead and ascended into heaven in his glorified humanity, he reconciles all things visible and invisible, and that all creation is therefore purposefully orientated, in and through him, towards the future revelation of the glorious liberty of God's children, when, in the new heavens and the new earth, there will no longer be death, mourning, sadness, or pain. Through Christ and through his life-giving Spirit, the Father creates and sanctifies, gives life, blesses, and bestows all good things.

Christians therefore cannot be pessimistic about the future of the world, nor believe in its periodic disintegration and renewal, both of which would deny Christ's future coming to judge the living and the dead, when he shall bring his recompense to repay everyone for what he has done. The god of the living will not destroy what he has created, but, in the future transformation of the world, he will reward the just and punish the evil.

This Gospel influenced the relationship of men and women to the environment through monastic institutions. Benedictine monks, especially inspired by their founder's evangelical sense of the stewardship of natural resources, advocated a harmonious union between prayer and work, between intellectual and physical effort, and between theoretical and practical skills.

This Good News produced a unique example of man's reconciliation with all creatures in St. Francis of Assisi, admired and invoked as the patron of ecologists and of those who are dedicated to the establishment of harmonious relations with the environment. Since God can express his will through all of his works, Francis was submissive to all creatures and scanned creation attentively, listening to its mysterious voices. In his "Canticle of Brother Sun" the saint called all creatures his brothers and sisters because they are God's gifts and signs of his providential and reconciling love. To God alone do they belong, to him they bear a likeness, and in his name Mother Earth, our sister, feeds us. In his personalized relationship with all creatures, St. Francis recognized his duty to reciprocate divine love with love and praise, not only in the name of creatures, but in, with, and through them.

For St. Francis, work was a God-given grace to be exercised in the spirit of faith and devotion to which every temporal consideration must be subordinate. All human effort in the world must therefore lead to a mutual enrichment of man and creatures.

Many are the causes of the ecological disaster which mankind faces today. Without pretending to be complete, the following should be singled out: uncontrolled use of technology for immediate economic growth, with little or no consideration for the planet's resources and their possible renewal; disregard for just and peaceful relations among peoples; destruction of cultures and environments during war; ill-considered exploitation of natural resources by consumer-oriented societies; unmastered and unregulated urbanization; and the exclusive preoccupation with the present without any regard for the future quality of life.

Therefore, in the name of Christ, who will come to judge the living and the dead, Christians repudiate:

- all forms of human activity — wars, discrimination, and the destruction of cultures — which do not respect the authentic interests of the human race, in accordance with God's will and design, and do not enable men as individuals and as members of society to pursue and fulfill their total vocation within the harmony of the universe;

- all ill-considered exploitation of nature which threatens to destroy it and, in turn, to make man the victim of degradation.

In the name of Christ, who will repay everyone for good works, Christians call upon all men and women to pursue:

- a synthesis between culture and faith;

- ecumenical dialogue on the goals of scientific research and on the environmental consequences of the use of its findings;

- the priority of moral values over technological advances;

- truth, justice, and the peaceful coexistence of all peoples.

16

RELIGIOUS COMMUNITIES

The most basic work of saving the Earth probably happens at the level of the community, one human at a time. Although politics and technologies are the levers people will use to forge the new human-Earth relationship, the will to use them for good requires motivation from the deepest levels of consciousness. Religious communities can be such a source of motivation for individuals, and ultimately for entire nations.

Upon learning that the crisis of the Earth is real, how can individuals learn to behave as if we know what we know? Realistically, what changes might we make in our thoughts and actions? How can one person counter the great monolithic consumer society facing people in the industrialized world? We can think these things through best with reinforcement from our communities, from friends, family, schools, churches, temples, and mosques. A religious community can offer a structure within which to contemplate and learn, and more than any other kind of institution, it can offer the moral authority for action.

Once we know what to do, we also need to gather with others to learn to amplify our voices and give greater power to our actions, so we can, for example, impress upon the commercial world that we don't need or want junk mail or excessive packaging, or persuade our governments to stop squandering the Earth's precious resources.

Following are four examples among many innovative and courageous faith communities that have taken steps to fulfill an environmental mission.

CATHEDRAL OF ST. JOHN THE DIVINE
1047 Amsterdam Avenue
New York, NY 10025

The Episcopal Cathedral of St. John the Divine, overlooking Harlem in New York City, has been at the forefront of the new global awareness since 1972, when James Parks Morton began his tenure as dean. The cathedral quickly became a center for new planetary ideas. Such shining lights in religion and science as Thomas Berry, René Dubos, Gregory Bateson, Lynn Margulis, and Buckminster Fuller were participants in cathedral programs in the early years. Here in 1979 James Lovelock gave the first public exposition of the Gaia hypothesis, the concept of the Earth as a living organism, which was soon to gain worldwide attention. The Gaia Institute was founded here in 1984 to explore implications of the Gaia hypothesis.

Global interfaith work has been a central mission for the cathedral. The magnificent Gothic structure is home to the Temple of Understanding, founded in 1960 with the encouragement of Pope John XXIII, the Dalai Lama, Thomas Merton, Eleanor Roosevelt, Jawaharlal Nehru, Anwar El Sadat, and Albert Schweitzer. Dean Morton, as president of the Temple of Understanding, has co-chaired two global conferences, at Oxford and

St. Francis Day celebration at the Cathedral of St. John the Divine, New York.
Photo: Mary Bloom.

Moscow, at which religious and political leaders from every continent and creed have considered the imperatives of a planetary perspective.

The Global Forum on Environment and Development took place in Moscow in 1990 at the invitation of President Gorbachev, the Supreme Soviet, the Soviet Academy of Sciences, and all the Russian faith communities. From that meeting, a document, drafted by scientist Carl Sagan, began a historic dialogue between scientists and religious leaders. The scientists' "Open Letter to the Religious Community" and the response from the religious leaders are included below (pp. 163, 166). These led to the founding of the Joint Appeal in Religion and Science for the Environment, headquartered at the cathedral.

A new environmental sermon series, "The Future of the Planet," began in 1978, continued with "Spiritual Energies of the Ecological Age, " in 1979, and the tradition has continued ever since. A celebration of the anniversary of the birth of St. Francis of Assisi takes place every year, highlighted by the now renowned Blessing of the Animals. Each year the parade of creatures great and small may include llamas, ponies, eagles, elephants, camels, giraffes, blue-green algae, and more.

The cathedral's Program for Environment is interwoven philosophically and practically with social justice work — feeding the homeless, working on housing issues, providing jobs and counseling for local youth. "Homes for the Homeless," a program the cathedral helped found, provided transitional housing for over two hundred of New York's homeless families in 1985. The 1987 Manhattan Valley Youth Outreach program put over a hundred inner-city foster care young people to work in New York's Morningside Park clean-up program.

The cathedral has served as the recycling center for the Upper West Side of New York for the past fifteen years. A series of Easter sermons called "Green New York" led to a process that gathered over two hundred New York environmental groups to produce a Green platform for the mayoral election. The cathedral is also a strong proponent and activist for Native American rights and religious freedom.

In the words of Dean Morton, "The understanding of humankind's place in the cosmos is always summarized and carried to its highest expression in a holy place, in a holy building."

NATIONAL CATHOLIC RURAL LIFE CONFERENCE
4625 N.W. Beaver Drive
Des Moines, IA 50310

With grassroots origins and a seventy-year history of ministry to rural Catholic America, the National Catholic Rural Life Conference (NCRLC) came early to social activism and concern with the Earth. The conference's traditional mission is to give Catholic and Protestant churches information on the environmentally sound management of church-owned agricultural and other land. This soon led to a broader concern for society's responsibility to sustain the environment and to its present core mission, which embraces the emerging ecological ethic of the 1990s.

NCRLC applies a hands-on approach to the protection and preservation of the environment, serving people in 170 Catholic dioceses. NCRLC also acts as a catalyst in environmental matters for the Catholic Church and helped the U.S. Catholic Conference to develop its recent national statement on the environment.

In the 1950s, NCRLC explored the moral dimensions of food and agricultural issues. In the 1970s the conference entered the public policy arena and drafted statements on land use, taxes, energy, and water. In the 1990s it has worked in areas ranging from soil erosion to global problems such as international trade negotiations, poverty, and development.

NCRLC is in the forefront of the new Catholic ecological awareness that Pope John Paul alluded to in his 1987 California speech and his January 1990 World Day of Peace speech, in which he declared that concern for the environment is a moral obligation.

In reformulating its core mission in May 1991, NCRLC committed to applying a fresh ecological ethic to its new twofold mission — the pursuit of justice in human relationships and the preservation of the integrity of God's creation. NCRLC's future will see increased involvement in food, agricultural, rural, and environmental issues.

SHOMREI ADAMAH
Church Road and Greenwood Avenue
Wyncote, PA 19095

Shomrei Adamah (Keepers of the Earth) is a community tied by shared interests rather than a geographical boundary. It is a growing Jewish community of nearly a thousand individuals and organizations across the United States and Canada. Members include affiliate groups and seminaries, individual students, rabbis, environmentalists, and youth. A small staff, led by director Ellen Bernstein, who founded the center in 1987, fields requests for information and support, serving as an international clearing house for people who want to understand and strengthen the link between Judaism and environmentalism.

Shomrei Adamah's mission is to inspire environmental awareness and practice among Jews by unlocking the treasure of ancient Jewish ecological wisdom. Judaism is a three-thousand-year-old tradition with strong ties to the land. The intellectual thrust is to link today's spirituality with its ancient origins. Shomrei Adamah works both ways: to bring the spiritual aspect to environmental issues, in the belief that the environmental crisis is partly a crisis of values, and to help bring environmental realties into the spiritual life of its members.

The organization provides a wealth of printed resources including authentic traditional sources, curricula, publications, speakers, and suggestions for creating a "green synagogue." A Jewish Environment Packet goes out to every member. A newsletter called "Voice of the Trees" comes out three times a year, detailing projects of member congregations and ways people can and do network together. Locally, Shomrei Adamah sponsors an All Species Day parade in its local community of Wyncote to celebrate Earth Day.

RIVERSIDE CHURCH
490 Riverside Drive at 122nd Street
New York, NY 10027

Leadership for spirituality and environmental activities came from within the congregation at Riverside Church. Dr. Frans C. Verhagen, an energy sociologist with divinity training from Dutch schools, joined Riverside in 1982 when William Sloane Coffin, controversial and widely respected for his disarmament and social justice work, was senior minister. Verhagen's Riverside Task Force on Ecological Stewardship became an official part of the church's Ecumenical Commission 1986.

Riverside Church, a beautiful Gothic structure patterned after the Chartres cathedral in northern France, is an interdenominational congregation of the American Baptist Church and United Church of Christ. Its membership is about three thousand and hails from all corners of the Earth.

A small dedicated group within this large, multifocused, interracial and international congregation developed a declaration called "Becoming an Earth Community Congregation" and helped set up energy efficiency, recycling programs, and bicycle parking. The task force considered the development of that declaration, still in draft form and reprinted below, as its major task, because members believe the specific social role of churches in the emerging ecological age is one of developing new values and vision to inspire and inform the environmental movement for the momentous task ahead.

In April 1990 Dr. Verhagen represented the Riverside Church at the World Council of Churches meeting in San Antonio, Texas, presenting a seminar titled "The Churches in the Ecological Age: Singing on the Titanic?" In May the Task Force together with the WCC U.S. Office and the Columbia University Chaplaincy organized the Riverside Conference on Becoming an Earth Community Congregation. Thomas Berry, Jay McDaniel, Danny Martin, Hazel Henderson, Paul Gorman, and others led workshops for 143 representatives of faith communities from fifteen states. Other such conferences are planned.

Riverside Church Declaration on Becoming an Earth Community Congregation

Preamble

The peril facing our planet comes not only from the threat of nuclear conflicts but also from the relentless destruction of life forms, life systems, planetary cycles, and energy flows.

While thousands of secular organizations and governmental institutions have sought to combat the environmental crisis, religious institutions have generally failed to give direction and vision in this area.

Riverside Church, which in the past gave national leadership to the disarmament and sanctuary movements, believes that hour has come to respond prophetically to the peril of ecological destruction so evident all around us. This statement is an attempt to begin a creative response.

1. *Acknowledging* that humans are part of and must be in union with all life forms and with all the Earth; and

2. *Realizing* the need for a spirituality of the Earth Community based on the biblical affirmation "The Earth is the Lord's" as well as other scriptural and non-scriptural religions and value systems; and

3. *Recognizing* that the injustice of gross affluence and gross poverty within and between nations is a major cause of ecological degradation; and

4. *Aware* that ecological and economic justice demands the Earth's bounty be shared among humans and between humans and other living beings; and

5. *Affirming* that the environmental crisis requires radical changes not only to public policy and institutional practices but also in individual behavior; and

6. *Mindful* that ecological stewardship requires a shift away from human centeredness to a culture in which care of the planet and its life is central;

The Riverside Church now declares itself an Earth Community Congregation, committed to preserving and cherishing the Earth. It agrees to develop an ecological spirituality of reconciliation between humans and the Earth, to practice ecological stewardship in the use of all its resources such as energy, supplies, investments, and to use its skills in education and advocacy to further ecological consciousness, responsibility, and commitment; and

Further the Riverside Church pledges to help other churches to become Earth Community congregations by sharing its experience, developing ecological liturgies and symbols, and organizing periodic educational events; and

Finally the Riverside Church will seek to contribute to the environmental movement a vision of the sacredness of the Earth and will join in formulating an environmentally oriented system of values and associated ethical standards for the emergent ecological age.

17

THE JOINT APPEAL
IN RELIGION AND SCIENCE

A HISTORICAL NOTE

Following are two statements, the first by leaders in science and the second a response by religious leaders. The documents are the results of a historic meeting of the minds of two spheres traditionally at odds with each other in a series of conferences. The first conference took place in January 1990, in Moscow, attended by scientific, spiritual, and political leaders from eighty-three nations. Sponsored by the Global Forum of Spiritual and Parliamentary Leaders, the conference began a process that culminated in the following "Open Letter to the Religious Community," signed by a group of distinguished scientists including several Nobel laureates and led by Dr. Carl Sagan.

Struck by the initiative, several hundred religious leaders of major faiths from five continents responded: "This invitation to collaboration marks a unique moment and opportunity in the relationship of science and religion. We are eager to explore as soon as possible concrete, specific forms of collaboration and action."

On June 2 and 3, 1991, a group of scientists and religious leaders again met, at the American Museum of Natural History and the Cathedral of St. John the Divine in New York, in a special summit sponsored by the Joint Appeal in Religion and Science. At this meeting and in response to the scientists' "Open Letter," these senior religious leaders of major American faith groups and denominations issued their "Statement by Religious Leaders at the Summit on Environment." Dr. Sagan called it "a courageous and historic commitment to cherish and protect the Earth by a broadly ecumenical gathering of American religious leaders. It affirms the joint responsibility of religious and political leaders, scientists, and citizens to work together to preserve the environment on which all our lives depend."

PRESERVING AND CHERISHING THE EARTH
An Open Letter to the Religious Community

The Earth is the birthplace of our species and, as far as we know, our only home. When our numbers were small and our technology feeble, we were powerless to influence the environment of our world. But today, suddenly, almost without anyone's noticing, our numbers have become immense and our technology has achieved vast, even awesome, powers. Intentionally or inadvertently, we are now able to make devastating changes in the global environment — an environment to which we and all other beings with which we share the Earth are meticulously and exquisitely adapted.

We are now threatened by self-inflicted, swiftly moving environmental alterations about whose long-term biological and ecological consequences we are still painfully ignorant: depletion of the protective ozone layer; a global warming unprecedented in the last 150 millennia; the obliteration of an acre of forest every second; the rapid-fire extinction of species; and the prospect of a global nuclear war which would put at risk most of the population of the Earth. There may well be other such dangers of which we are still unaware. Individually and cumulatively, they represent a trap being set for the human species, a trap we are setting for ourselves. However principled and lofty (or naive and shortsighted) the justifications may have been for the activities that brought forth these dangers, separately and taken together they now imperil our species and many others. We are close to committing — many would argue we are already committing — what in religious language is sometimes called "Crimes Against Creation."

By their very nature these assaults on the environment were not caused by any one political group or any one generation. Intrinsically, they are transnational, transgenerational, and transideological. So are all conceivable solutions. To escape these traps requires a perspective that embraces the peoples of the planet and all the generations yet to come.

Problems of such magnitude, and solutions demanding so broad a perspective, must be recognized from the outset as having a religious as well as a scientific dimension. Mindful of our common responsibility, we scientists — many of us long engaged in combatting the environmental crisis — urgently appeal to the world religious community to commit, in word and deed, and as boldly as is required, to preserve the environment of the Earth.

Some of the short-term mitigations of these dangers — such as greater energy efficiency, rapid banning of chlorofluorocarbons, or modest reductions in nuclear arsenals — are comparatively easy and at some level are already underway. But other, more far-reaching, long-term, and effective approaches will encounter widespread inertia, denial, and resistance. In this category are conversion from fossil fuels to a nonpolluting energy economy, a continuing swift reversal of the nuclear arms race, and a voluntary halt to world population growth — without which many other approaches to preserve the environment will be nullified.

As with issues of peace, human rights, and social justice, religious institutions can be a strong force here, too, in encouraging national and international initiatives in both the private and public sectors, and in the diverse worlds of commerce, education, culture, and mass communications.

The environmental crisis requires radical changes not only in public policy, but also in individual behavior. The historical record makes clear that religious teaching, example, and leadership are able to influence personal conduct and commitment powerfully.

As scientists, many of us have had profound experiences of awe and reverence before the universe. We understand that what is regarded as sacred is more likely to be treated with care and respect. Our planetary home should be so regarded. Efforts to safeguard and cherish the environment need to be infused with a vision of the sacred. At the same time, a much wider and deeper understanding of science and technology is needed. If we do not understand the problem, it is unlikely we will be able to fix it. Thus, there is a vital role for both religion and science.

We know that the well-being of our planetary environment is already a source of profound concern in your councils and congregations. We hope this appeal will encourage a spirit of common cause and joint action to help preserve the Earth.

Carl Sagan
Cornell University
Ithaca, New York

Hans A. Bethe
Cornell University
Ithaca, New York

Elise Boulding
University of Colorado
Boulder, Colorado

M. I. Budyko
State Hydrological Institute
Leningrad, U.S.S.R.

S. Chandrasekhar
University of Chicago
Chicago, Illinois

Paul J. Crutzen
Max Planck Institute for Chemistry
Mainz, West Germany

Margaret B. Davis
University of Minnesota
Minneapolis, Minnesota

Freeman J. Dyson
Institute for Advanced Study
Princeton, New Jersey

Affiliations for identification purposes only

Richard L. Garwin
IBM Corporation
Yorktown Heights, New York

Gyorgi S. Golitsyn
Academy of Sciences of the U.S.S.R.
Moscow, U.S.S.R.

Stephen Jay Gould
Harvard University
Cambridge, Massachusetts

James E. Hansen
NASA Goddard Institute for
    Space Studies
New York, New York

Mohammed Kassas
University of Cairo
Cairo, Egypt

Henry W. Kendall
Union of Concerned Scientists
Cambridge, Massachusetts

Motoo Kimura
National Institute of Genetics
Mishima, Japan

Thomas Malone
St. Joseph College
West Hartford, Connecticut

Lynn Margulis
University of Massachusetts
Amherst, Massachusetts

Peter Raven
Missouri Botanical Garden
St. Louis, Missouri

Roger Revelle
University of California, San Diego
La Jolla, California

Walter Orr Roberts
Yorktown Heights, New York
National Center for Atmospheric Research
Boulder, Colorado

Abdus Salam
International Centre for Theoretical Physics
Trieste, Italy

Stephen H. Schneider
National Center for Atmospheric Research
Boulder, Colorado

Nans Suess
University of California, San Diego
La Jolla, California

O. B. Toon
NASA Ames Research Center
Noffett Field, California

Richard P. Turco
University of California
Los Angeles, California

Yevgeniy P. Velikhov
Academy of Sciences of the U.S.S.R.
Moscow, U.S.S.R.

Curl Friedrich von Weizsacker
Max Planck Institute
Starnberg, West Germany

Sir Frederick Warmer
Essex University
Colchester, United Kingdom

Victor F. Weisskopf
Massachusetts Institute of Technology
Cambridge, Massachusetts

Jerome B. Wiesner
Massachusetts Institute of Technology
Cambridge, Massachusetts

Robert R. Wilson
Cornell University
Ithaca, New York

Alexey V. Yablokov
Academy of Sciences of the U.S.S.R.
Moscow, U.S.S.R.

STATEMENT BY RELIGIOUS LEADERS
AT THE SUMMIT ON THE ENVIRONMENT

On a spring evening and the following day in New York City, we representatives of the religious community in the United States of America gathered to deliberate and plan action in response to the crisis of the Earth's environment.

Deep impulses brought us together. Almost daily, we note mounting evidence of environmental destruction and ever-increasing peril to life, whole species, whole ecosystems. Many people, and particularly the young, want to know where we stand and what we intend to do. And, finally, it is what God made and beheld as good that is under assault. The future of this gift so freely given is in our hands, and we must maintain it as we have received it. This is an inescapably religious challenge. We feel a profound and urgent call to respond with all we have, all we are, and all we believe.

We chose to meet, these two days, in the company of people from diverse traditions and disciplines. No one perspective alone is equal to the crisis we face — spiritual and moral, economic and cultural, institutional and personal. For our part, we were grateful to strengthen a collaboration with distinguished scientists and to take stock of their testimony on problems besetting planetary ecology. As people of faith, we were also moved by the support for our work from distinguished public policy leaders.

What we heard left us more troubled than ever. Global warming, generated mainly by the burning of fossil fuels and deforestation, is widely predicted to increase temperatures worldwide, changing climate patterns, increasing drought in many areas, threatening agriculture, wildlife, the integrity of natural ecosystems, and creating millions of environmental refugees. Depletion of the ozone shield, caused by human-made chemical agents such as chlorofluorocarbons, lets in deadly ultraviolet radiation from the sun, with predicted consequences that include skin cancer, cataracts, damage to the human immune system, and destruction of the primary photosynthetic producers at the base of the food chain on which other life depends. Our expanding technological civilization is destroying an acre and a half of forest every second. The accelerating loss of species of plants, animals, and microorganisms which threatens the irreversible loss of up to a fifth of the total number within the next thirty years, is not only morally reprehensible but is increasingly limiting the prospects for sustainable productivity. No effort, however heroic, to deal with these global conditions and the interrelated issues of social justice can succeed unless we address the increasing population of the Earth — especially the billion poorest people who have every right to expect a decent standard of living. So too, we must find ways to reduce the disproportionate consumption of natural resources by affluent industrial societies like ours.

Much would tempt us to deny or push aside this global environmental crisis and refuse even to consider the fundamental changes of human behavior required to address it. *But we religious leaders accept a prophetic responsibility to make known the full dimensions of this challenge, and what is required to address it, to the many millions we reach, teach, and counsel.*

We intend to be informed participants in discussions of these issues and to contribute our views on the moral and ethical imperative for developing national and international policy responses. But we declare here and now that steps must be taken toward: accelerated phaseout of ozone depleting chemicals; much more efficient use of fossil fuels and the development of a non-fossil-fuel economy; preservation of tropical forests and other measures to protect continued biological diversity; and concerted efforts to slow the dramatic and dangerous growth in world population through empowering both women and men, encouraging economic self-sufficiency, and making family education programs available to all who may consider them on a strictly voluntary basis.

We believe a consensus now exists, at the highest level of leadership across a significant spectrum of religious traditions, that the cause of environmental integrity and justice must occupy a position of utmost priority for people of faith. Response to this issue can and must cross traditional religious and political lines. It has the potential to unify and renew religious life.

We pledge to take the initiative in interpreting and communicating theological foundations for the stewardship of Creation in which we find the principles for environmental action. Here our seminaries have a critical role to play. So too, there is a call for moral transformation, as we recognize that the roots of environmental destruction lie in human pride, greed and selfishness, as well as the appeal of the short-term gain over the long-term.

We reaffirm here, in the strongest possible terms, the indivisibility of social justice and ecological integrity. An equitable international economic order is essential for preserving the global environment. Economic equity, racial justice, gender equality, and environmental well-being are interconnected and all are essential to peace. To help insure these, we pledge to mobilize public opinion and to appeal to elected officials and leaders in the private sector. In our congregations and corporate life, we will encourage and seek to exemplify habits of sound and sustainable householding — in land use, investment decisions, energy conservation, purchasing of products, and waste disposal.

Commitments to these areas of action we pledged to one another solemnly and in a spirit of mutual accountability. We dare not let our resolve falter. We will continue to work together, add to our numbers, and deepen our collaboration with the worlds of science and government....

It has taken the religious community, as others, much time and reflection to start to comprehend the full scale and nature of this crisis and even to glimpse what it will require of us. We must pray ceaselessly for wisdom, courage, and creativity. Most importantly, we are people of faith and hope.

These qualities are what we may most uniquely have to offer to this effort. We pledge to the children of the world and, in the words of the Iroquois, "to the seventh generation," that we will take full measure of what this moment in history requires of us. In this challenge may lie the opportunity for people of faith to affirm and enact, at a scale such as never before, what it truly means to be religious. And so we have begun, believing there can be no turning back.

June 3, 1991, New York City

Bishop Vinton R. Anderson
President, World Council of Churches

Rabbi Marc D. Angel
President, Rabbinical Council of America

The Most Reverend Edmond L. Browning
Presiding Bishop and Primate of the
   Episcopal Church

Reverend Joan Campbell
General-Secretary
National Council of Churches of Christ

The Reverend Herbert W. Chilstrom
Bishop
Evangelical Lutheran Church in America

Father Drew Christiansen, S.J.
Director
Office of International Justice and Peace
United States Catholic Conference

Ms. Beverly Davison
President, American Baptist Church

Reverend Dr. Milton B. Efthimiou
Director of Church and Society
Greek Orthodox Archdiocese of North
   and South America

Bishop William B. Friend
Chairman of the Committee for Science
   and Human Values
National Conference of Catholic Bishops

Dr. Alfred Gottschalk
President, Hebrew Union College–
   Jewish Institute of Religion

Dr. Arthur Green
President
Reconstructionist Rabbinical College

His Eminence Archbishop Iakovos
Primate, Greek Orthodox Archdiocese of
   North and South America

The Very Reverend Leonid Kishkovsky
President
National Council of Churches of Christ

Chief Oren Lyons
Chief of the Turtle Clan of the Onondaga
   Nation

Dr. David McKenna
President, Asbury Theological Seminary

The Very Reverend James Parks Morton
Dean, Cathedral of St. John the Divine

Dr. W. Franklyn Richardson
General Secretary
National Baptist Convention

Dr. Patricia J. Rumer
General Director, Church Women United

Dr. James R. Scales
President Emeritus
Wake Forest Theological Seminary

Dr. Robert Schuller
Pastor, The Crystal Cathedral

Dr. Robert Seiple
President, World Vision, U.S.A.

Bishop Melvin Talbert
Secretary of the Council of Bishops
United Methodist Church

Dr. Foy Valentine
Former Executive Director
Christian Life Commission
Southern Baptist Convention

Affiliations for identification purposes only

18

THE EARTH SUMMIT

❧

The International Coordinating Committee on Religion and the Earth (ICCRE) is an organization of spiritual groups and individuals dedicated to promoting global awareness of the truth that the environmental crisis is at heart a spiritual crisis. ICCRE's founder and director is Rev. Daniel Martin of Wainwright House (260 Stuyvesant Avenue, Rye, NY 10580), an interdenominational study center. Rev. Martin is a religious consultant to the United Nations Conference on Environment and Development (UNCED), and from 1986 to 1988 he gained international recognition for his work on the Environmental Sabbath with the United Nations Environment Programme. ICCRE has been a catalyst in producing the following Earth Charter, written as an expression of a combined global religious voice of concern for the Earth, with input from North American, Asian, African, and Latin American religious leaders.

This Earth Charter will be presented as the religious contribution to the final document of the UNCED meeting in June 1992 in Rio de Janeiro, Brazil. Preceding the Earth Charter is an introductory essay by Rev. Martin.

A RELIGIOUS VOICE FOR THE EARTH
by Rev. Daniel Martin

In the last two centuries the human has emerged as the dominant organism of the Earth, impacting the very Earth process, which involves every other life-system. In a matter of years we are destroying what required millions of years of formation by the Earth community. The urgency of our crisis can hardly be exaggerated. Scientists speak of a window of thirty to fifty years before we render our situation irreparable. Our time-frame is the lives of our own children.

The basic task before us is the creation of a new set of principles out of the ruined condition of our world: norms of an "Earth justice" that will foster the vitality and continuing evolutionary unfolding of the planet. In order for that to happen, we humans must realize our planetary and cosmic dimensions, that we are, in fact, the conscious mode of evolutionary unfolding.

To discover these principles we turn to the whole process of cosmic unfolding, to the great body of knowledge gleaned from human attempts to understand the nature of life.

The New Cosmology for a New Consciousness

Today, in the midst of our chaos, we are experiencing the emergence of the story of life — its origins, its process, and our participation in its emergence. It is the story that links us to all creation. In its midst, a new consciousness is emerging.

In human history, consciousness has emerged in great bursts: in Egypt five thousand years ago the pyramids symbolized human preoccupations with mortality; in India three thousand years ago the sacred Veda captured new insights about life; twenty-five hundred years ago in Israel, Greece, India, and China marvelous individuals emerged to shape the souls of human beings; two thousand years ago Jesus of Nazareth initiated a movement that impacted subsequent western history; fifteen hundred years ago, the prophet Mohammed gave new direction to the Arab world; a thousand years ago in the West, the vision of the Middle Ages grew out of the School at Chartres Cathedral; five hundred years ago in the Academy of Florence, Renaissance humanism was forged.

Today we are in the throes of just such a burst of consciousness. Out of the world of science — the traditional enemy of religion — the foundations of a new story are being forged, that the universe itself is a story and that its unfolding is *the* primary sacred event.

Today, science gives us the basis of a new story in which our story is seen to be both part of Earth's story and part of God's story. Our dust is stardust, our family tree has intergalactic branches. This is a new story of the oneness and interconnectedness of all life, where everything we do affects everything else. We are part of everything, so that "to pluck a flower is to trouble a star."

This miracle of creation is clearly not staged for our benefit alone. We are part of an unfolding mystery that has been going on for 16 billion years. Our species is the most recent child of this process. In the clock of the universe, we appear on the scene only seconds before the midnight hour.

For the first time we actually have a common history of the universe, in which humans appear as the self-expression of the whole, the universe in a conscious mode. It is this cosmic history that will provide the context for the transformation of consciousness that is already happening and that many anticipate will break out soon as a planetary phenomenon. In order to become the myth that will direct our world, however, this transformed consciousness will have to involve all of us: your experience and mine; the stories of millions. All are expressions of the one story of creation.

When the visions of oneness and interconnectedness converge with the facts of empirical science, we will know again where we are, who we are, and how we should fit into the cosmic scheme.

These visions are found today among the artists and poets, the naturalists and the "deep ecologists," and within the developing ecofeminist perspective. The religious traditions of the world are replete with insights into the oneness and sacredness of all life. This is particularly true of the indigenous cultures. Often, however, these insights were unable to surface in a culture that was dualistic and mechanical, exploitative and destructive of the Earth.

The Role of Religion

Religion has a special role and responsibility in this whole process, for religion is what calls us back to who we are, by telling us the story of life. The religious traditions of the world are filled with wisdom, and with intuitions forged from long experience of life and human nature. But religion itself, as institution, is founded and constructed upon our basic assumptions about reality. These assumptions have begun to shift, moved by the crises they have caused and re-directed by the discoveries of human science. Religion, therefore, will undergo a radical reformulation, a cosmicization of its own traditions and insights.

Already, in fact, in the various religious traditions we find glimpses of the sort of future that we seek for ourselves and our children. Thus, in the indigenous world, there is the example of sustainable living, as well as the sensitivity that sees the Earth as alive. In a similar way, the Hindu tradition has a deep sense of divine manifestation: the world is alive with the presence of many gods.

In terms of human living, the goal of Shinto practice is life in harmony with nature and with others. It is based on a proper sense of gratitude toward nature. The ancient Taoist wisdom defines the human as *hsin* — the mind and heart of the universe. Buddhist teaching proclaims that we can attune ourselves to this harmony by living lives of gratitude and service. For the Jewish world, the meaning of life is to be found in limits, in how we relate to God, to the natural world, and to other human beings. Judaism contains a strain of self-denial, forcing us to remember that our domination is only partial. For the Christian, the change of self occurs through practicing praise, thanks, repentance, and by asking and receiving forgiveness, and loving God and others in daily life. The Moslem tradition emphasizes the need to rediscover the sacred, for the visible world is not an independent order of reality but a manifestation of a vastly greater world which transcends it and from which it issues. The Baha'i vision stresses the unity of material and spiritual evolution. Humanity is part of the communion of life while the evolution of civilization is part of a planetary process.

Religion is the paramount storyteller that links us to one another, to creation, and to God. In the new context — undergirded by the new cosmology — new religious sensitivities emerge that not only expand the appreciation of traditional insights, but also, thereby, give birth to a meta-religion: a new reality that is born of the communion of the traditions. This reality is not so much another religion, formed out of the merging of many perspectives, as something that stands beyond the sum of its parts. In fact, one aspect of this meta-religion is the enrichment of each of the traditions. It is the union of lovers, the unity that fosters diversity.

Out of such a unity can come the special kind of inspiration and direction that the religious world can offer to our present time of crisis: a common statement of principles, a collaboration for deeper understanding, a joining of forces for effective action. The United Nations Conference on Environment and Development (UNCED) offers an opportunity for such combined effort. The UN conference is asking the religious world to help in the creation of an Earth Charter, which it sees to be in the tradition of the Universal Declaration of Human Rights; only, this time, raised to a new level to embrace the rest of creation.

EARTH CHARTER
A Global Religious Contribution

Preamble

The crisis we face today is a spiritual one:

> We have forgotten who we are,
> we have lost our sense of wonder and connectedness,
> we have degraded the Earth and our fellow creatures,
> *and we have nowhere else to go.*

At the same time, partly because of this crisis, we are also experiencing a new global awareness and the rediscovery of traditional wisdom, confirmed now by the findings of science. For the first time in our history, we have empirical evidence for a common creation story in which everything is connected to everything else, so that:

> if we lose the sweetness of the waters, we lose the life of the land,
> if we lose the life of the land, we lose the majesty of the forest,
> if we lose the majesty of the forest, we lose the purity of the air,
> if we lose the purity of the air, we lose the creatures of the Earth,

not just for ourselves,
but for our children,
both now and in the future.

If we are to preserve this delicate balance of life for our children, we must commit to:

- a transformation of our hearts and minds

- concrete changes in our way of life.

If our religions are to be relevant and effective, we must commit to:

- the reformulation of our traditional insights.

If we are to realistically address our problems, be they environmental or social, educational or economic, and enter a new era of creativity, we must commit to:

- the development of a global perspective and approach supported by global institutions.

TODAY

We remember who we are.
We reclaim our sense of wonder and connectedness.
We rejoice in what we can be.
We celebrate the Earth.

Spiritual Principles

Unity and Diversity. The Earth community is a complex, interdependent system and can survive only in its integral and interconnected functioning. All the diverse parts of the system are essential to its functioning and beauty.

Humility. Our relationship to the Earth must be one of humility. Care for the Earth must be a serious concern of every human institution, profession, program, and activity.

Equity. Life is a gift, given equally to all. It must be treated with respect and with due consideration of others, including future generations.

Rights and Responsibilities. Every human being has the right to a healthy environment in which to live. But human beings also have a special responsibility to preserve life in its integrity and diversity, within the parameters of the ecological system, and to avoid the wanton destruction of anything for trivial or merely utilitarian reasons.

Beauty. The beauty of the Earth is food for the human spirit: it informs human consciousness. The beauty of the Earth is the source of human creativity: it inspires the imagination with awe and wonder, it fires the soul of the artist.

Ethics for Living

Sustainably. Human development must be fostered in a way that meets the needs of the present without compromising the ability of future generation to meet their own needs.

Justly.

Sufficiently:
In a world of great disparities between rich and poor, justice demands that everyone be able to obtain sufficient sustenance and a decent standard of living.

In Participation:
Universal participation, including that of women and minorities, in all aspects of a sustainable society, must be facilitated by legal and institutional measures.

In Solidarity:
Balanced and integrated growth will only be achieved through the widespread adoption of values and ethics which give primacy to global solidarity, including the rights of future generations.

Frugally. In order to establish economic justice, humans in the developed world must learn to live more simply.

Peacefully. Consultation, leading to constructive resolution, must replace confrontation and domination in the relations between nations. The effects of war on the environment, as well as on the human population, become increasingly disastrous, while the production of weapons stresses the Earth's resources and pollutes the life-support systems.

Interdependently. A new Earth order, guided by universally agreed upon and enforceable regulations, is essential to carry out the changes demanded by a global society.

Knowledgeably. Universal education is key to nurturing global awareness and ecological knowledge among the world's citizens.

Holistically. Progress, to be authentic, must include the improvement of the individual's moral, spiritual, physical, and intellectual condition, within a community context.

Programs

Our concern for all life expresses itself not only in our prayers and in statements of principles, but in actions in our personal, professional, and political lives. We, representatives of the world religious communities, recommend the following actions to create a society that is socially just and ecologically sound, and we call upon our members to implement them in their personal and professional lives.

1. Redistribute the ownership and control of the land, wealth and natural resources of the Earth, so that the many who have too little are provided with the basic necessities for a full life. This will require a restructuring of the present economic system that includes the promotion of "quality of life indicators," rather than simply measures of quantity, and addresses the issue of debt and world trade agreements.

2. Stabilize the world's population. (We recognize that a child born in a materially privileged society will consume and pollute many times as much as one born in poverty. We recognize also that reducing birth rates requires education and economic opportunity for the poor — particularly women.)

3. Promote patterns of individual and organizational consumption that are sustainable, emphasizing:

    a. Where practicable, eating lower on the food chain and eating food that is organically, humanely, and locally produced.

    b. Buying products that last. Recycling. Conserving.

    c. Minimizing the use of fossil fuels.

    d. Investing only in companies with a demonstrated commitment to ecological principles and practices (e.g., the Valdez Principles).

4. Develop religious education in our own systems that promotes awareness of the ecological consequences of daily action. Such education would focus, not only on the pollution and destruction of the life-support systems of the Earth and social injustice, but on the spiritual and psychic consequences of participating in a materialistic and exploitive cultural system.

5. Create rituals and celebrations that honor the Earth and encourage its protection:

    a. Set aside a day at least monthly and possibly weekly for a special practice of living lightly on the Earth (e.g., minimal use of fossil fuels for transportation, etc.), and for spiritual enrichment (e.g., music and storytelling, meditation and prayer, folk festivals, Councils of All Beings, etc.): a day for "being" rather than "having."

    b. Celebrate such a day worldwide, once a year. The United Nations Conference on Environment and Development (UNCED) meeting in Brazil in 1992 would offer a unique opportunity for exemplifying and teaching this practice, as well as building political support for a serious Earth-saving effort by UNCED.

6. Promote the development of an Earth-centered curriculum for public schools which would be grounded in the rhythms and cycles of nature and would cultivate an understanding and love of all life. Encourage all public and community organizations to include such an ecological agenda in their programs.

7. Promote the protection of remaining habitats (forest, wetlands, rivers, estuaries, etc.) through wilderness preservation and sustainable life practices.

8. Contribute to the ethical process involved in the development and application of biotechnology and genetic engineering.

9. Promote the development of safe alternatives to nuclear energy.

10. Promote the reduction of weapons spending and the arms trade.

11. Promote the limitation of the power of transnational corporations. Encourage their enormous ability to effect justice and sustainable development.

12. Preserve and strengthen the voices of the oppressed, particularly women, indigenous people, the poor, and other species.

13. Promote creative alternatives to development through indigenous knowledge in addition to science-based knowledge.

14. Encourage support of politicians who work for policies that foster sustainable life.

15. Support the creation of an international "environmental watch" organization.

Postscript

Since we, the authors of this statement, are people born into privilege, we recognize that our recommendations reflect this perspective and are directed toward what we and others like us best can do to embody a deeply ecological religious faith. While many of the recommendations apply to all people, they do so with varying degrees of priority and implication. We hope that our bias will be supplemented by those of others, so that we can arrive, ultimately, at a balanced and effective Earth Charter.

THE EARTH SUMMIT
The United Nations Conference
on Environment and Development, UNCED*

A number of forces led to the call for a United Nations Conference on Environment and Development by the UN General Assembly in the fall of 1989. First was an interest by the international community in developing a "report card" on the progress of national governments in the area of environment since the Conference on Environment in Stockholm in 1972. As governments began to consider new international treaties, conventions, and codes, they realized the need to review the data from each country regarding environmental assessments, measurements, and legal instruments.

Also, the two-year study by the Brundtland Commission provided a strong case for the consideration of issues of the environment and development together in the context of sustainable development, as outlined in the book *Our Common Future*. However, it became clear early that southern governments would not participate in an environment conference unless the issues of development were considered. The Brundtland report helped to frame the upcoming debate in an environment and development context. United Nations Resolution 44/228 states that the conference "should elaborate strategies and measures to halt and reverse the effects of environmental degradation in the context of strengthened national and international efforts to promote sustainable and environmentally sound development in all countries." It is from this charge that all subsequent preparations for UNCED flow. Additionally, it is especially important that provisions have been made for the participation by NGOs (non-governmental organizations) in all aspects of the complex preparations for UNCED. This includes input into the substantive reports being prepared by the UNCED Secretariat as well as NGO access to the meetings of the Preparatory Committee of UNCED.

The major results of UNCED are expected to be the following:

- Three or four new conventions (treaties)
- A charter of rights (Earth Charter)
- An agenda for the twenty-first century (Agenda 21)
- A redefinition of roles and responsibilities for various UN agencies

---

*"The Earth Summit" is reprinted with permission of its author, Michael McCoy, and with thanks to the Global Tomorrow Coalition.

The issues that will be discussed at UNCED include:

- Climate change
- Transboundary air pollution
- Deforestation
- Desertification
- New/renewable energy sources
- Ozone layer
- Marine pollution
- Living marine resources
- Freshwater
- Education/information
- Poverty and environmental degradation

- Toxic waste disposal
- Urban environment
- Environment and health
- Financial resources
- Biodiversity
- Technical transfer
- Biotechnology
- Institutions
- Economic instruments
- Legal aspects

The conventions that are expected to be signed in Brazil include:

- Climate change (Global warming/greenhouse gases)
- Biodiversity
- Forests
- Biotechnology

Earth Charter

The charter of rights, or what is now being referred to as an "Earth Charter," will be a magna carta on the required relationships between environment and development. It is seen by the UNCED Secretariat as a "moral framework," the foundation upon which sustainable decisions on environment and development can be made. It would guarantee the rights of countries in the South to continue to pursue their policies of economic development but within a prescribed set of conditions that will not threaten planetary "environmental security." At the same time it would safeguard against destructive practices by the North. It will be the ethical standard underlying the actions outlined in Agenda 21.

Agenda 21

The second key output of the United Nations Conference on Environment and Development 1992 will be what is referred to as Agenda 21. This will be the environment/development agenda for the next century and will provide the framework for institutional modification to be accomplished over the next decade. Agenda 21 is expected to be developed from all sectors of society and, in turn, impact all sectors of society. The implementation schedule is expected to be from 1993 to 2000.

Agenda 21 will set out strategies to coordinate efforts regionally and globally. It will identify the policies necessary to create the required environment/development linkages. It will recommend new environmental laws to preserve the ecological balance of the planet and will set out a specific action plan for drought and desertification. It will contain recommendations on ways and means of integrating environment and economy and identify ways of providing new financial resources. Perhaps most importantly, it will address the difficult issues of the transfer of environmentally sound technology throughout the world and the related questions regarding the development of human resources. It will recommend, where appropriate, changes to international infrastructure including the strengthening of the environmental capacity of existing United Nations agencies and institutions. It will also set out recommendations regarding improvements in education and information transfer.

. . . in Parting

❀

When we talk about global crisis, or a crisis of humanity, we cannot blame a few politicians, a few fanatics, or a few troublemakers. The whole of humanity has a responsibility because this is our business, human business. I call this a sense of universal responsibility. That is a crucial point.

So, brothers and sisters, if you agree with some of these thoughts, please try to implement them as well as to explain them to other brothers and sisters. If you do not feel they are very useful, then just forget it! No problem. Thank you very much.

— His Holiness, the XIVth Dalai Lama, in "Universal Responsibility and a Global Approach to Peace," address to the Global Survival Conference, Oxford, 1988

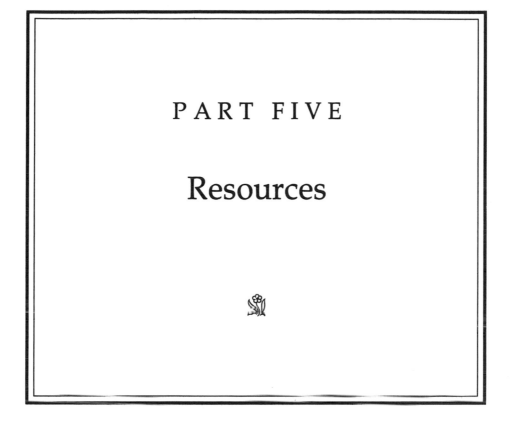

PART FIVE

Resources

BOOKS

Environmental Crisis

Andruss, Van, and Christopher Plant, Judith Plant, and Eleanor Wright, eds. *Home! A Bioregional Reader.* Santa Cruz, Calif.: New Society Publishers, 1991.

Brown, Lester, et al. *State of the World: A Worldwatch Institute Report.* 1987, 1988, 1989, 1990, 1991. New York: W. W. Norton, 1987–91.

Barney, Gerald. *The Global 2000 Report to the President of the United States Entering the Twenty-First Century.* 3 vols. New York: Pergamon, 1984.

Brundtland, G. H. *Our Common Future.* New York: Oxford University Press, 1987.

Corson, Walter H., ed., and the Global Tomorrow Coalition. *The Global Ecology Handbook: What You Can Do about the Environmental Crisis.* Boston: Beacon Press, 1990.

Ehrlich, Paul R. *The Population Bomb.* New York: Ballantine, 1968.

Ehrlich, Paul R., and Anne H. Ehrlich. *The Population Explosion.* New York: Simon and Schuster, 1990.

Environmental Protection Agency. *The Environmental Consumer's Handbook.* Municipal and Industrial Waste Division, EPA, 401 M Street, S.W., Washington, DC 20460.

Lovelock, James E. *The Ages of Gaia: A Biography of Our Living Earth.* New York: W. W. Norton, 1988.

McKibben, William. *The End of Nature.* New York: Random House, 1989.

Meadows, Donella H. *The Global Citizen.* Covelo, Calif.: Island Press, 1991.

Myers, Norman. *Gaia: An Atlas of Planet Management.* New York: Doubleday, 1984.

National Academy of Sciences. *Policy Implications of Global Warming.* Washington, D.C.: U.S. Government Printing Office, 1991.

OECD. *The State of the Environment,* 2001 L Street, N.W., Suite 700, Washington, DC 20036.

Sadik, Nafis. *The State of World Population 1991.* New York: United Nations Population Fund, 1991.

Seredich, John, ed. *Your Resource Guide to Environmental Organizations.* Irvine Calif.: Smiling Dolphins Press, 1991.

Silver, Cheryl Simon, and Ruth DeFries. *One Earth, One Future: Our Changing Global Environment.* National Academy of Sciences. Washington, D.C.: National Academy Press, 1990.

World Resources Institute, United Nations Environment Programme, and United Nations Development Program. *World Resources 1990–1991: A Guide to the Global Environment.* New York: Oxford University Press, 1990.

Religion and the Environmental Crisis

Berry, Thomas. *The Dream of the Earth.* San Francisco: Sierra Club Books, 1988.

Berry, Thomas. *The Riverdale Papers,* vols. 1–10 and continuing. Riverdale Center, 5801 Palisade Avenue, Bronx, NY 10471.

Fox, Matthew. *Original Blessing: A Primer in Creation Spirituality.* Santa Fe, N.M.: Bear & Company, 1983.

Granberg-Michaelson, Wesley. *A Worldly Spirituality: The Call to Redeem Life on Earth.* New York: Harper & Row, 1984.

Hall, Douglas. *Imaging God: Dominion as Stewardship.* Grand Rapids: Eerdmans, 1986.

Lewis, Thomas. *The Lives of a Cell: Notes of a Biology Watcher.* New York: Bantam Books, 1975.

Lonergan, Anne, and Caroline Richards, eds. *Thomas Berry and the New Cosmology.* Mystic, Conn.: Twenty-Third Publications, 1987.

McFague, Sallie. *Models of God: Theology for an Ecological, Nuclear Age*. Philadelphia: Fortress Press, 1987.

Moltmann, Jürgen. *God in Creation: A New Theology of Creation and the Spirit of God*. San Francisco: Harper & Row, 1985.

Presbyterian Church, USA. *Restoring Creation: For Ecology and Justice*. Louisville, Ky.: Office of the General Assembly, Presbyterian Church, 1990.

Roberts, Elizabeth, and Elias Amidon, eds. *Earth Prayers from around the World*. New York: HarperCollins, 1991.

Sahtouris, Elisabet. *Gaia: The Human Journey from Chaos to Cosmos*. New York: Pocket Books, 1989.

Scherff, Judith S. *The Mother Earth Handbook: What You Need to Know and Do — At Home, in Your Community, and through Your Church — To Help Heal Our Planet Now*. New York: Continuum, 1991.

Seed, John, and Joanna Macy, eds. *Thinking Like a Mountain: Towards a Council of All Beings*. Philadelphia: New Society Publishers, 1988.

Spretnak, Charlene. *The Spiritual Dimension of Green Politics*. Santa Fe: Bear & Company, 1989.

Spretnak, Charlene, and Fritjof Capra. *Green Politics: The Global Promise*. Santa Fe: Bear & Company, 1989.

Swimme, Brian. *The Universe Is a Green Dragon: A Cosmic Creation Story*. Santa Fe: Bear & Company. 1984.

Teilhard de Chardin, Pierre. *The Phenomenon of Man*. New York: Harper & Row, 1959.

Turner, Frederick. *The Western Spirit against the Wilderness*. New York: Viking Press, 1980.

ORGANIZATIONS

Center for Respect of Life and
Environment
2100 L Street, N.W.
Washington, DC 20037
(202) 452-1100
Contact: Rick Clugston

Eco-Justice Working Group
National Council of Churches
475 Riverside Dr.
New York, NY 10155
(212) 870-2483
Contact: Dean Kelly

Fellowship in Prayer
291 Witherspoon Street
Princeton, NJ 08542

The Green Hotline: (800) 435-9466
Joint Appeal in Religion and Science
Cathedral of St. John the Divine
1047 Amsterdam Avenue
New York, NY 10025

ICCRE
International Coordinating Committee
on Religion and the Environment
Wainwright House
260 Stuyvesant Avenue
Rye, NY 10580
(914) 967-6080
Contact: Rev. Daniel Martin

IMPACT
100 Maryland Avenue, N.E.
Washington, DC 20002
(202) 544-8636
Contact: Gretchen Eick

Interfaith Coalition on Energy
P.O. Box 26577
Philadelphia, PA 19141
(215) 635-1122

Louisiana Coastal Wetlands Interfaith
Stewardship Plan
c/o First United Methodist Church
P.O. Box 2039
Lafayette, LA 70502
Contact: Sarah Schoeffler

NACRE (North American Coalition on
Religion and Ecology)
5 Thomas Circle
Washington, DC 20005
(202) 462-2591
Contact: Diane Sherwood

North American Conference on Christianity
and Ecology
444 Waller Street
San Francisco, CA 94117

United Nations Environment Programme
Room DC2-803
United Nations
New York, NY 10017
(212) 963-8139

West County Toxics Coalition
1019 McDonald Avenue
Richmond, CA 94804
(415) 232-3427

World Wildlife Fund Network on
Conservation and Religion
10 rues des Fosses
CH-1110 Morges, Switzerland

DENOMINATIONAL OFFICES

American Baptist Churches, U.S.A.
P. O. Box 851
Valley Forge, PA 19482
(215) 768-2495
Contact: Andy Smith

Episcopal Church Center
815 Second Avenue
New York, NY 10017
(212) 867-8400

Friends in Unity with Nature
608 E. 11th Street
Davis, CA 95616
Contact: Chris Laning

National Spiritual Assembly of the Baha'is
of the United States
Office of External Affairs
1606 New Hampshire Avenue, N.W.
Washington, DC 20009
(202) 265-8830
Contact: Jeff Huffines

Presbyterian Church (U.S.A.)
Committee on Social Witness Policy
100 Witherspoon Street
Louisville, KY 40202-1396
(502) 569-5809
Contact: William Somplatsky-Jarman

Shomrei Adamah
Church Road and Greenwood Avenue
Wyncote, PA 19095
(215) 887-1988
Contact: Ellen Bernstein

Union of American Hebrew Congregations
Religious Action Center of Reformed
Judaism
2027 Massachusetts Avenue, N.W.,
Washington, DC 20036
(202) 387-2800

United Church of Christ
Commission for Racial Justice
105 Madison Avenue
New York, NY 10016
(212) 683-5656
Contact: Charles Lee

United Methodist General Board of Church
and Society
Ministry of God's Creation
100 Maryland Avenue, N.E.
Washington, DC 20002
(202) 488-5650
Contact: Jaydee Hanson/Paz Artaza

United States Catholic Conference
3211 4th Street, N.E.
Washington, DC 20017
(202) 5431-3000
Contact: Walter Grazer

The following sources are gratefully acknowledged...

"Earth's average temperature rise" (chart, p. 30): From Walter H. Corson, ed., and the Global Tomorrow Coalition, *The Global Ecology Handbook: What You Can Do about the Environmental Crisis* (Boston: Beacon Press, 1990). Data based on James E. Hansen, "The Greenhouse Effect: Impacts on Current Global Temperature and Regional Heat Waves," in Dean Edwin Abrahamson, ed., *The Challenge of Global Warming* (Washington, D.C.: Island Press, 1989), and Richard A. Warrick and Philip D. Jones, "The Greenhouse Effect, Impacts and Policies," *Forum for Applied Research and Public Policy*, Fall 1988; as published in Christopher Flavin, *Slowing Global Warming: A Worldwide Strategy*, Worldwatch Paper 91 (Washington, D.C.: Worldwatch Institute, October 1989), 18.

"Rise in concentration of CO_2 in the atmosphere" (chart, p. 30): From C. D. Keeling et al., "A Three Dimensional Model of Atmospheric CO_2 Transport Based on Observed Winds: Observational Data and Preliminary Analysis," Appendix A, in *Aspects of Climate Variability in the Pacific and the Western Americas*, Geophysical Monograph, vol. 55, Nov. Copyright © 1989 by the American Geophysical Union.

Thomas Berry, for "The Spirituality of the Earth."

Timothy Weiskel, for "Doing Theology on a Small Planet," first published in *Harvard Divinity Bulletin* 19, no. 3 (Fall 1989).

Carl Sagan and Paul Gorman (Cathedral of St. John the Divine) for "Preserving and Cherishing the Earth: An Open Letter to the Religious Community" and "Statement by Religious Leaders at the Summit on Environment."

"A Prayer for Conservation," by Patricia Winters, in the United Nations Environment Programme's Environmental Sabbath information kit.

"Everything Is Sacred," by Dr. Mohammed Mehdi, Secretary General, National Council on Islamic Affairs, in the United Nations Environment Programme's Environmental Sabbath information kit.

Ellen Bernstein, director of Shomrei Adamah, an international resource center for Jewish perspectives on the environment, for "Forging a New Land Ethic from the Bible."

"The Earth Is at the Same Time Mother" "I am the One," and "A Prayer of Awareness," by Hildegard of Bingen, reprinted from *Meditations with Hildegard of Bingen*, by Gabriele Uhlein, copyright 1983 Bear & Co., Inc., by permission of Bear & Co., Inc. PO Drawer 2860, Santa Fe, NM 87504.

"Be a Gardener," by Julian of Norwich, reprinted from *Meditations with Julian of Norwich*, edited by Brendan Boyle, copyright 1983 Bear & Co., by permission of Bear & Co., Inc. PO Drawer 2860, Santa Fe, NM 87504.

Robert A. White, "Spiritual Foundations for an Ecologically Sustainable Society," *Journal of Baha'i Studies* (Ottawa) 2, no. 1.